THE
NON-BEARDY
BEER BOOK

THE
NON-BEARDY
BEER BOOK

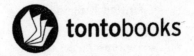 tontobooks

www.tontobooks.com

Published in the UK in 2008 by Tonto Books Ltd
Copyright © Tonto Books Ltd 2008
Edited by Paul Brown & Stuart Wheatman
All rights reserved
The moral rights of the authors have been asserted

ISBN-13: 9780955632648

British Library Cataloguing in Publication Data:
A catalogue record for this book is available
from the British Library

Printed and bound in the UK by
CPI Cox & Wyman, Reading, RG1 8EX

Tonto Books
Newcastle upon Tyne
United Kingdom

www.tontobooks.com

Contributors: Dave Amos (DA), Paul Brown (PB), Hazel
Cameron (HC), Simon Gallagher (SG), Mark Jones (MJ),
W David Leighton (WDL), David Lynn (DL), Rob Meddes
(RM), Jamie Rothwell (JR), Nicolas Sheffield (NS), Gary
Taylor (GT), Trampjuice (TJ), James Watson (JW),
Malcolm Watson (MW), Stuart Wheatman (SW)

NOTES

Beers are presented in the following format:

BRAND NAME
UK distributor
Country of origin, Percentage alcohol by volume (ABV)

The top ten icon denotes a UK bestseller.

Country of origin is not necessarily the same as the country of manufacture.

Alcohol by volume (ABV) percentages can vary.

Scottish & Newcastle was acquired by a consortium of Carlsberg and Heineken in April 2008. At the time of going to press it had been announced that Heineken would acquire S&N UK.

The information in this book is correct to the best of the authors' knowledge at the time of publication.

The opinions expressed in this book are those of the individual authors and do not necessarily reflect the views of the publisher.

Please drink responsibly...

CONTENTS

INTRODUCTION

Beer. The inspiration for our wildest dreams and the mastermind behind our most spectacular gaffes; what would life be without that accidental one-too-many? But how much do we actually know about our liquid nemesis, the delicious golden poison we pour down our necks most nights and every other lunchtime? Thanks to the concerted, elitist and bewildering efforts of our friendly neighbourhood connoisseur, probably very little. And how much do we actually care? Even less, you could say. After all, who needs another lug-full of the depressingly familiar 'tasting notes' cribbed from *The Beer Bore's Book of Bluster*? Can they really *all* have a velvety mouth feel and a grassy nose? Do frothy heads come in any colour except white? The question could be asked: isn't it time there was a book written by normal people who wouldn't know a long finish with hops and toasted malt from a happy finish with sticky belly in the flat above the takeaway, and who are perfectly happy with that? *The Non-Beardy Beer Book* aims to change things a little with a comprehensive and irreverent guide to the nation's favourite drink, calling 'time gentlemen, please' on the tedious real ale buff in the corner, hunched over his half of warm, flat sheep dip and his dog-eared jotter. Things you most definitely won't find in here: any gargling, hocking, or sluicing. Nor will there be any sweaters, sandals, or stout yeomen of the bar. And, as the title of this book so defiantly says, there'll be no whopping great beards, especially ones full of food and phlegm and fugitives from justice. Instead there's a whole host of fascinating and pertinent facts about the UK's most popular brands, liberally smothered in a layer of smart-arse remarks and topped with amusingly tangential nonsense. The reviews have been put together through a hung-over fuzz by folk who simply like to have a beer or two, wrestle with the odd belligerent lamppost on the way home, and then get up the next morning and do it all again. We believe they're all the qualifications and equipment that anyone could possibly need for a definitive guide to beer, and can guarantee that our writers have nothing so much as an internet-bought tasting diploma between them, let alone an overflowing spittoon. As well as being an essential companion for an adventurous pub-crawl, *The Non-Beardy Beer Book* is also an indispensable guide to a quiet night in with the telly. Whether you're mulling over an attractive gift set with a funny-shaped tankard in a luxury supermarket, or peering through the bulletproof glass in a problem estate off-licence, there'll be something in here to point you in the right direction. And if the only thing that's stopping you from blowing an hour's wages on a bottle of something exotic in your local pretentious lounge bar is its pronunciation, our polyglot team might just have had an educated stab at that for you too. How's that for service? *MJ*

AMSTEL

Heineken UK
Netherlands, 5.0% ABV

Amstel, or 'Am-shtel' to give its correct Dutch pronunciation, is the little beer brother of Heineken. It is named after the river in the Netherlands that runs through the north of Amsterdam, where the Amstel Brewery was founded in 1870. The brewery was taken over by Heineken in 1969 – a smart move when you consider by this time Amstel was already a worldwide brand with its own breweries located in Suriname, Jordan, the island of Curaçao, Puerto Rico and Greece. It was first exported to the UK in 1883, and is currently available in over 75 countries. Heineken moved production of the beer to Zoeterwoude in 1982, so Amstel is now produced 30 miles outside of Amsterdam. The beer itself is smooth and malty yet rather watery – surprising, as it is a decent strength 5% ABV pilsner style lager. Keeping the H_2O theme going, while we Europeans get to drink Amstel brewed using fresh clean spring water, the Amstel brewery on Curaçao produces the only beer in the world that is made with 100 percent seawater – desalinated of course. The labels on the bottles have used the famous red and gold colour scheme since first production in 1870. There is a different coat of arms for each variation of Amstel, all based on the city of Amsterdam's crest. So drink up and dispose of your empties correctly – Amstel's brown bottles are apparently the most recycled in the world. *GT*

ASAHI

Shepherd Neame
Japan, 5% ABV

The Asahi Beer Hall is one of Tokyo's most notable modern landmarks and serves as a symbol for the Asahi Beer Company at the location where they have been making beer for over a century. The building was put together by swanky designer Philippe Starck and, with its black granite exterior topped off with a shiny gold flame-like structure, it looks to be the perfect headquarters for this achingly trendy brand. A symbol of style over substance? Hmm... The lager first came to light in this country in the late 80s and early 90s when it could regularly be found splashed across the pages of the style press with glossy ads taken out in the likes of *The Face* and *ID* magazines. It was a period when style slaves stopped drinking lager of a generic variety and needed to be seen with a branded drink so as not to detract from the brilliance of their vastly over-priced trousers. In short, it was one of the first designer lagers, and people went along with the notion that, if something comes from Japan, it must be cool. That's the style, but what about the substance? Its 'super dry' taste is admittedly fairly crisp but it has something of a metallic after-taste which is prone to linger, as if you'd been licking a robot for a while. Such an unsavoury image hasn't stopped Asahi from becoming the top-selling Japanese lager in the UK. (Pub quiz: If you can name the second top-selling Japanese lager in the UK, without the help of Google, I'll get the next round in.) *RM*

BALTIKA

Scottish & Newcastle
Russia, 5.1% ABV

In trendy new bars up and down the land, condensation-beaded bottles are dispensed from their own icy cold bar-top fridge, the metallic blue and silver label with the name Baltika engraved in that mystical Cyrillic typeface drawing you in. The promise of Russian mystique coupled with those heady days of Glasnost conjures up thoughts of friends with rosy cheeks, clinking glasses all enjoying a night out together in big furry hats. Baltika produce nine numbered beers, and they've selected number three – Russia's bestseller – with which to tempt us Brits. Once tasted, though, there's no getting away from the fact that Baltika number three is pretty much the Steve Davis of bottled beers: bland and weirdly dry with an non-refreshing aftertaste. A few bottles of Baltika left me feeling like I'd been done over by a Muscovite prostitute, which, let me tell you, does not make for a pleasant experience. Perhaps the trouble is that any Russian product, especially beer, will struggle to seem fresh, invigorating, vibrant or particularly drinkable to Western punters. Instead, we're conjuring up images of Stalag-like industrial towns, queues for beetroot, and dogs being rocketed to a certain death in space. Crucially, by jumping on the imported beer bandwagon, and advertising itself as a fresh new modern brand with Trafalgar Square launch parties and glamorous scantily-clad girls, the bods behind Baltika have forgotten that decent taste counts for a lot. My advice? Stick to vodka. That's something the Russians are undeniably good at. *GT*

BASS
InBev
UK, 4.5% ABV

Is Bass the 'artiest' of all beers? There's certainly a case for it. Multiple cases of the stuff, in fact. While the likes of Beck's and Stella Artois have tried to bask in the reflected glory of Damien Hirst, Tracey Emin and the rest of the young British daubers, with various sponsorship deals, Bass beers have actually featured in many famous paintings. The most famous is probably Manet's Bar at the Folies-Bergès which depicts a bored looking barmaid standing behind a row of champagne and Bass bottles. The beer can also be seen in over 40 paintings by Picasso which he knocked together in the early 1900s. Over 40? Paint what you love, I say. Bass also cropped up in one of Quentin Blake's illustrations for the Roald Dahl children's book *The Twits*. But why has Bass become such a muse for so many artists? It's all about that iconic logo. The Bass logo (a red triangle) was the first trademark ever to be registered in Britain – back in 1876 – and consequently become a shorthand way for any artists wanting to depict an ale; just shove a red triangle on a bottle and there you have it: Bass beer. The ubiquitous triangle still adorns 'the original pale ale' and signals a drink which is nicely balanced not too sweet, not too dry, and with the kind of legacy that'll soon have you wanting to emulate the lifestyle of the 20th century's great cubists (without the one-legged, syphilitic prostitutes, naturally). *RM*

BECK'S
InBev
Germany, 5% ABV

I remember the day I discovered Beck's with great fondness. I say remember, it's all quite hazy after drink number five, but what remains in my mind is the realisation that Beck's is a decidedly regal lager – some might call it the real king of beers. I affectionately flirted with the bottled variety earlier in my drinking career, but never committed to moving away from the familiarity of Stella or the swoon-making satisfaction of Heineken until I spotted that Beck's was available on tap. From that moment, Beck's became the first name on the team sheet on a night out. I found myself swerving towards bars in whose doorways I would not normally pause to urinate, drawn by the glistening silver pump. Why? Aside from the obvious downright moreishness of the thing – proven by the fact that many people, including myself, are repeatedly willing to shell out upwards of three pounds for the stuff – the taste is unrivalled. It's a slice of Bremen perfection, peripherally sweet and fruity, but with a body that would make a nun blush. It blitzes down the throat shouting *Achtung Schweinehund!* and *Schnell!* making powerful Bavarian love to the taste buds. And you can definitely tell it's not from 'round here' – it's zingy and pleasurably metallic, borne of water that has not been flavoured with abandoned shopping trolley. Beck's is remarkable in so many ways – notably that it inspires poetic adjectives in men who usually eat kebabs on Tuesdays. Sober. *SG*

BECK'S ALCOHOL FREE
InBev
Germany, 0.05%

Hmm... Non-alcoholic lager. There's a weird notion to contemplate while staring into the bottom of an empty glass and not feeling in the slightest bit tipsy. Rather like 'government intelligence' or 'overjoyed goth', non-alcoholic lager is something of an oxymoron with 'non-alcoholic' and 'lager' not appearing to be particularly happy bedfellows. I mean, why would anyone really choose to drink lager unless it was guaranteed to give them that warm fug of well-being (before the inevitable slide into self-loathing)? And just who is it aimed at? Drivers tired of Coke? Pregnant women tired of tomato juice and Tabasco? Anyone tired of life? Having said that, Beck's Alcohol Free certainly looks the part. It comes in the same kind of green glass bottles that 'normal' Beck's lager comes in and when you pour it out looks very similar to the real stuff, too. But rather than brewing it as a normal beer and then removing all the alcohol, Beck's simply doesn't add yeast to the mix of hops, water and malted barley so that it never ferments. The resultant taste is rather 'hoppy', and there is something of a lingering sweetness, but it is, nevertheless, as close as you're going to get to lager without actually sticking any alcohol in it. Think of it as a *Stars In Their Eyes* version of Beck's: looks bona fide, but on closer inspection is just a watered-down version of the real deal, and not particularly satisfying on a Saturday night. *RM*

BECK'S VIER
InBev
Germany, 4% ABV

Drinkers in continental Europe must surely chuckle as they recline in their chairs by the canal, crack jokes surrounded by four generations on the sun glazed terrace, or even wobble off their bicycles in sheer mirth at us useless, feeble British boozers. Only in a nation that allowed an advertising campaign describing Carlsberg as 'probably the best lager in the world' (akin to describing a city council dry ski-slope as 'a genuine rival to Val-d'Isere') would the powers that be take a perfectly decent German pilsner and decide to do almost nothing with it except make it very slightly weaker for lily-livered Brits. Beck's has been ticking along just fine for 135 years, hinting that it's doing something right. And it is – it's crisp, it's clean... but that's another review. This tastes fairly similar, if – obviously – a little weaker, but, really, why? The original tastes nicer and is only one percent stronger. It is hardly like drinking meths. Stick five pints down you and you'll feel a bit drunk. Likewise here. Beck's didn't really need a weaker younger sibling, but it's got one to its own detriment. There's nothing really bad about it from a taste perspective, I'll admit that. It's a German pilsner, so surprises are not really in the offing. But original Beck's was a decent pint, and you'll be even harder pressed to track it down on tap now that it's been usurped by this Vier stuff, which is a real shame. *DA*

BLACK SHEEP ALE

Black Sheep Brewery
UK, 4.4% ABV

If you have any doubts about dipping into something connected with sheep, then don't. This is a first-rate bitter – crisp and with a good head to lace your glass. If ever proof was required that competition is good for consumers, then this must be it. The small North Yorkshire village of Masham has two breweries owned by different branches of the same family, and both the Theakston's and Black Sheep breweries manage to produce excellent and successful beers. This one, along with some more unusual brews, including the famous Holy Grail (named in tribute to Monty Python and recently presented to the Pope by the Archbishop of York), is brewed in antique vessels that have been restored by the fifth generation of the family. It is also fermented in the Yorkshire Square system developed over 200 years ago, and this produces a distinctive and full-bodied ale, with a strong, smooth and bitter taste. I first enjoyed it at the brewery in Masham after an informative tour where you can watch the brewing process and be wafted off your feet by the smell of the boiled wort (the combination of malted grains boiled with hops). I also like the design of the bottles – this one has a nice label with a black sheep, and clearly states the ingredients – simple and informative. Bottles of Black Sheep are now widely available in many major supermarkets, which is handy if you can't make a round trip to North Yorkshire. *HC*

BLACKTHORN CIDER

Constellation
UK, 5.5% ABV

Blackthorn used to be a dry cider called, funnily enough, 'Blackthorn Dry Cider'. Now it's a sweet cider, the recipe changed and only the brand name remaining, presumably to help snag a bite of the cider revolution apple. So what does 'Ice Cold Filtered' Blackthorn Cider offer that Magners, Bulmers, Woodpecker and indeed the Constellation-owned Gaymer Company's own Gaymer's Original does not? I'm struggling to come up with anything other than rather attractive bar towels. Blackthorn recently enjoyed a £3 million relaunch, which saw it receive a rocktastic new logo that looks a bit like heavy metal T-shirt design and doesn't seem like a particularly good fit with the accompanying slogan 'The taste of the West Country'. I'm not really a regular cider drinker – not since my teenage years – but I do know that cider is supposed to be made from apples. You wouldn't discern this from Blackthorn's taste, tolerable, but with a sharp metal twang when drunk from a can. Perhaps they're only using the pips. Its colouring is darker than expected, not the bright golden colour you'd imagine from a cider, but that hardly counts as a unique selling point. The name Blackthorn brings back some unpleasant memories – I once had a blackthorn splinter slip into my finger that caused great pain and eventual poisoning. My experience of drinking Blackthorn Cider will be much easier forgotten. Years ago, the blackthorn bush was known for its medicinal qualities. Perhaps Blackthorn Cider will one day be known for its medicinal taste. *HC*

BODDINGTONS

InBev
UK, 3.8% ABV (4.1% cask)

Most things Manchester is renowned for are no longer bound to the city. Manchester United is owned by Americans, floppy haircuts are found in trendy bars up and down the country, Morrissey has moved to Los Angeles, and Boddingtons – the city's most famous beer – is brewed in Wales. Strangeways, Manchester's home of porridge-eaters and mailbag-stitchers, was also home to the Boddingtons brewery for over 220 years. Conglomerate Interbrew (now part of InBev) saw it fit to move production to the valleys of South Wales in 2005, refusing to take into account the fact that the original brewery drew water from the Ardwick fault 200 feet below. Aficionados say the resultant new brew is not a patch on the malty smooth and surprisingly quaffable former version. A cask edition is still produced in the city, although not at the original site, therefore retaining the thinnest of grips on its Mancunian heritage. In typical Manchester style, the original brewery has taken on a new lease of life as a nightclub and music venue. If you look carefully at the Boddingtons logo you'll notice two bees sitting on a barrel. Often appropriated to the two 'B's of 'Boddingtons Beer' or the yellow and black colour scheme, the bees actually represent Manchester's status as a 'hive' of industry during the industrial revolution. (Considering the fact that former bra model Melanie Sykes famously advertised the beer, perhaps double 'D's would be more appropriate.) Boddingtons, the cream of Wales, boyo! *GT*

BOHEME

Tesco
Czech Republic, 4.7% ABV

Boheme is an own-brand lager from Tesco, and can be cheaper to buy than a bottle of own-brand water. This, you'd think could be a warning sign, but don't be put off – it tastes pretty darn good when compared to the usual bland, fizzy mixes available from UK supermarkets. Most likely this is because it is brewed in the Czech city of České Budějovice by Budějovický Mestansky Pivovar (BMP), who produced the original Budweiser in 1802. The brewery tell us in their marketing spiel that it is brewed with the same recipe, ingredients and methods originally used in the 1800s – although I have an inkling that it's been watered down a bit. The legal battle over the use of the Budweiser trademark is a 100-year-old hot potato that is covered in more depth in the following Anheuser-Busch Budweiser and Budějovický Budweiser Budvar reviews. Although BMP could confidently argue that they have the right to use the 'Budweiser' name, Tesco have sensibly sidestepped the issue and labelled Boheme as a 'Pilsen'. It's a nice light apricot colour, with a medium body and is quite bitter but sweet on the palate, the taste is not very complex and leaves you with a somewhat doughy, malty aftertaste but it is refreshing enough. There is a lot of bubbling going on, but it doesn't drink 'fizzy'. It will pass the taste test if you're managing on a budget and need to entertain friends who enjoy a decent beer. *HC*

BRAHMA
InBev
Brazil, 4.8% ABV

First created in Brazil in 1888, the first thing that is noticeable about this pale lager is its uniquely-shaped bottle. Basically, it is designed to fit snugly in your hand to enhance the drinking experience. Enjoyment is the priority here. Brahma encompasses the Brazilian philosophy called 'ginga'. In the UK, of course, ginga is something occasionally shouted at unfortunate ginger-haired people, but the Brazilians are much more civilised than that. An African word that found its way to Brazil through a dance/martial art called Capoeira, ginga (pronounced *jin-ga*) means never taking life too seriously and always being free-spirited. Other than capturing that in the bottle's design, that's what they want us to get from the beer's taste. I'm not saying you immediately want to do the Samba, but it will certainly put you on the road to having a time. It's not too gassy and is a drink to be savoured and appreciated, rather than rammed down the throat. It's light, yet strong, and perfect if ice cold, either at home or in the pub. But you'll have to be quick – InBev relegated Brahma from their 'core drive brand lagers' in summer 2008. A poor result for a promising 2005 £5 million signing. The stars in the Brahma logo are inspired by the stars that were visible in the sky above Rio on the day the republic of Brazil was declared. Brahma would get five more stars if I was awarding them, but as I'm not, I recommend you give this one a try and discover a new meaning for ginga. *SW*

BUDWEISER
Anheuser-Busch
USA, 5.0% ABV

Whassup?! WHASSUP?! The self-proclaimed 'King of Beers' entertained students and office grunts alike with that hilarious phrase for all of five minutes in the 1990s courtesy of a series of phone prank-based TV commercials. And then there were the 'Bud-Weis-Er' frogs. Huge marketing campaigns have made Budweiser the ever-present beer in UK bars and offies. All-American Bud is the Coca-Cola of beers, with an iconic bottle design that has barely changed since the stuff was first brewed in 1876. But what does it taste like? Man alive, it's fizzy. Drink this fast and you could belch the *Star Spangled Banner* with ease. But I'm not sure it actually *tastes* of anything. A cold one is refreshing, sure, but most cold beers can make that claim. Let's file it under 'refreshingly bland'. If you want less fizzy, you need to head over to Bud Ice. Another spin-off brand, Bud Silver – a 'European-style beer with a fuller premium flavour' specifically marketed at UK drinkers – seems to have been discontinued. Americans can choose from no less than eight Budweiser brands, the latest of which is Bud Chelada, 'a blend of Budweiser and Clamato juice'. Clamato juice is tomato juice mixed with clam broth. I'm going to stick my neck out and say that particular spin-off is unlikely to reach this side of the Atlantic. Czech beer Budweiser Budvar is most definitely NOT a Budweiser spin-off – see that beer's entry, and the long-running legal battle between Anheuser-Busch and Budějovický Budvar. *PB*

BUD ICE
Anheuser-Busch
USA, 5.5% ABV

Thank the lager Gods! Another Bud on the market, but not just a lame, weaker, superfluous counterpart. The difference here is in the brewing process. It's chilled to just below freezing point, making ice crystals form in the beer. Being a fan of Budweiser, I was a bit hesitant at trying this. I mean, Bud is the king of beers – why would you want to tamper with something so perfect? Bud Ice is a lot lighter than Bud in taste and texture and feels a lot more invigorating. One thing that sometimes gets me about Bud is how gassy it is, so Ice was a welcome improvement. Reluctantly, I gave in and enjoyed this lager. It provided all the enjoyment of Bud, with the added excitement of trying something newer and edgier. This is another lager that is all about progress – they've improved a product and shown a great sense of detail. The bottle is well designed, making it appear more dynamic, like the go-getter son of the old-timer, out to prove himself and make his mark in the big bad world of lager. He's different, he's a trend-setter, he's got the looks, chirpier personality, the better packaging, refined taste, he's the lager of the future. The king is dead. Long live the new king of beers! For the odd session or two, anyway. I dare say Bud Ice was introduced to provide a different Bud experience, a nice change, somewhat snazzier, but probably not something you'd leave the old faithful for. *SW*

BUDWEISER BUDVAR
Budějovický Budvar
Czechoslovakia, 5.0% ABV

This Czech premium lager is not to be confused with the US Budweiser – brewers Budějovický Budvar and Anheuser-Busch have been embroiled in a trademark dispute for the best part of a hundred years. Budweis is a town in Germany famed for independent beer breweries, and 'Budweiser' is an adjective meaning 'in the style of Budweis', much as 'Pilsner' means 'in the style of Pilsen'. In Europe, both Budvar and Anheuser-Busch use the 'Budweiser' name. In the US and Canada, an agreement between the two brewers means that Budvar is sold as Chechvar, and distributed by Anheuser-Busch. The legal arguments, however, continue. So that's the name, but what about the beer? In a taste-test, Czech Budvar beats US Bud hands-down, mainly by virtue of actually having a flavour. It's also a proper beer according to the Bavarian Reinheitsgebot Purity Law. (US Bud contains rice, and therefore doesn't qualify.) No 'Whassup!'-style nonsense from Budvar, either, although the blurb on its website is twaddle of the highest order. 'You can taste Budweiser Budvar Czech Premium Lager with all your senses,' it claims. 'First of all you will delight your eyes with its beautiful colour and rich dense foam, then you will feel the fine aroma of the hops, in your palm you will stroke the dewy glass and, in the end, you will taste the fine to medium strong bitterness. You will remember well, our perfect lager.' Actually, as marketing twaddle goes, that's deceptively effective. It doesn't half make me fancy a cool pint of Budvar. *PB*

BULMERS ORIGINAL

Scottish & Newcastle
UK, 4.5% ABV

Surely it will go down as one of the greatest product relaunches ever – the noughties cider-over-ice revolution. Formerly banished to the abandoned roundabouts and swings of desolate inner-suburb parks, cider was rescued and reinvented as a splendidly-chilled complement to a fine summer's afternoon. But behind the ingeniously simple idea of making cider sexy by pouring it from pint bottles over ice lies a quagmire of legal wrangles involving international markets, patents, market shares, and lots and lots of apples. Let's clear up one thing straight away – Bulmers and Magners are not the same thing. Unless you're in Ireland. Confused? Basically, the Bulmers Original brand is owned by C&C in Ireland and S&N in the UK. So when C&C decided to launch Bulmers in the UK in 1999, they changed its name to Magners. Then, when S&N entered the cider-over-ice market in 2006, they launched their new drink as Bulmers. So Magners is Bulmers and Bulmers is something else entirely, unless you're in Ireland, where Bulmers is Bulmers and Magners doesn't exist. Anyone else's head hurting? One thing is clear – with sales of both brands rocketing, it's a cider war out there. It's Bulmers versus Magners, with Bulmers being the underdog – and we all know that the Brits love an underdog as much as a few crafty bevvies. Sadly, Bulmers' flavour is contrived and commercialised almost as if it were made from those plastic apples that sit in furniture showrooms. It's enjoyable, though anything but original. *JW*

CAFFREY'S

Coors
UK, 4.2% ABV

The brilliantly-named Clotworthy Dobbin was a famous brewer in 19th century Belfast, and, had he not married off his daughter to Thomas Caffrey, drinkers might still be asking for pints of 'Dobbin's'. As it is, Thomas Caffrey built a bigger brewery and claimed the family business as his own. The rest is beer-swilled history. The distinctive 'fruitiness' of the Caffrey's beer was first brewed in the 1950s using a yeast developed by renowned Irish 'brewing scientist' Brian Gilliland. The beer – and the brewery – has had a fairly turbulent recent history. The Caffrey's brand name was revived in the 1990s when the brewery was purchased by Bass. But when Bass sold out to Interbrew in 2004, Caffrey's brewery was closed. Interbrew later sold the distribution rights to Coors, who initially appeared to be trying to kill off the brand by ending distribution to the US. Yet Caffrey's remains one of the UK's bestselling 'ales', largely due to a successful foray into the ever popular 'extra cold' market. It can be bought in a nitro widget can, which gives it a good thick head. The beer itself has a creamy texture and slight caramelised malty flavour. I suspect the original recipe is no longer used – certainly the ABV has dropped from 4.8% to 4.2%. Caffrey's is considered one of the Irish red beers and has a slightly red tinge, but there are better red ales with a more ruby colouring and superior taste.
HC

CARLING

Coors
UK, 4.1% ABV

No beer brand sums up the recent change in UK drinking habits more than Carling. Twenty years ago, Carling Black Label ruled the fag-ash pubs of Britain, alongside fellow no-frills lagers like Skol, Harp and Hofmeister. Landlords took little care of their generic draughts, pumping them through neglected pipes and selling them cheap. If drinkers did have a favourite, their choice was likely influenced by entertaining ads, such as those featuring Carling's classic 'I bet he drinks Carling Black Label' slogan (or Hofmeister's much-missed pork pie hat-wearing George the bear). A lot has changed. The fag-ash pubs are luxury bars, lagers are sold at a premium as 'extra cold' or with a slice of lime, Hofmeister has disappeared, and the market is dominated by big (relatively) exotic brands like Stella, Foster's and Bud. But Carling has flourished, dropping the 'Black Label', offering Extra Cold and Creamflow Premier varieties, and slugging it out at the very top of the list of the UK's biggest selling beers. Notably, Carling jumped aboard the 1990s 'lad culture' bandwagon personified by *Loaded* magazine and Oasis, sponsoring the Premiership and music events, and offering cheeky, way-hey, lads together, advertising. Today, Carling is very much the *Nuts* and Razorlight of British lagers – undeniably popular, relatively inoffensive, but pretty darn unexciting. Funnily enough, Carling pretends to be British, but is owned by Americans and was born in Canada. Kind of like a beery equivalent of Owen Hargreaves. *PB*

CARLING C2

Coors
UK, 2% ABV

If ever a lager was created by people without the slightest idea of what drinkers want then this is it. A bland, inoffensive-tasting pint that – yes – will quench your thirst if your throat is dry, but come on, so will a cup of tea. And Carling C2 is *two* percent proof. That's only half as strong as Foster's, which in turn is only half as strong as Duvel, which the Belgians can cope with just dandy without all hell breaking loose. Carling calls it a 'mid-strength' lager, but fans of Tennent's Super or Special Brew might disagree. So what is the point of Carling C2? Does it have a particularly compelling taste? Of course not – the fact that the word 'Carling' is in the name should tell you all you need to know about that. And this, Carling claim, is the result of ten years of research involving almost 1,000 recipes. 'We can't say exactly how it's done,' say Carling, 'or anyone with a mash tin and a lifetime of brewing experience would be at it.' Ten years of effort to come up with something that is effectively a brand-name shandy? In other news, cancer remains uncured. Carling's 'master brewers' have wasted their time, and if you buy C2 you'll be wasting yours. The fact that in recent adverts C2 happens to be a robot's tipple of choice tells you all you need to know, I'm afraid. I'm human, and I'd probably reach for the engine oil before sinking one of these. *DA*

A Non-Beardy Guide to ALCOPOPS

First-time drinkers were once required to 'develop a taste' for ales and bitters that, on first sup, tasted like the Devil's own home brew. But it was a rite of passage that had to be negotiated by pretending you actually liked the stuff until, one glorious day, you actually did. Alcopops have made a mockery of such rituals, being a kind of safety net for first-time drinkers who are growing up refusing to touch anything that is harsher on the palette than Lilt. Let's start our rundown of top alcopop brands with **WKD**. Their adverts ask: 'Have you got a WKD side?' and feature a bunch of identikit 'pub blokes' playing practical jokes on each other. The trouble is, these blokes invariably act like the type of goons that would have you beating a path out of the pub door the minute you clocked eyes on their non-hilarious antics. And here's another thing: what self-respecting, proper 'bloke', is going to be seen dead ordering a bottle of WKD anyway? They come in a variety of sugary flavours all tasting like alcoholic sherbet dib-dabs. Speaking of 'blokes', **Barcadi Breezer** is apparently now Cockney rhyming slang for 'geezer'. Ironic really seeing as you're more likely to catch proper geezers extolling the virtues of avant-garde shadow puppetry than swigging from a bottle of this stuff. No, when it comes to discovering what type of person has made the Breezer into one of the most popular alcopops in the country you have only to check out the social net-working site, Facebook. Click on someone's page and have a look at the photographs they have posted up there. If

there are any snaps of a gaggle of women in a bar, one or more of the group will almost certainly be waving a bottle of Barcadi Breezer around their heads in an apparent show of wild abandon. Yep, this rum-based alcopop is a hit with the party-girl-about-town and it comes in a variety of poppy flavours. **Archers Aqua** (a clear mix of schnapps and fruit drink) purports to be made especially for the upmarket, female drinker and, hey girls, guess what? It's better for you as it contains 30% less sugar than many other alcopops (in the same way that one cake is better for you than two cakes). **VK** is short for Vodka Kick and is apparently a big favourite with clubbers. Having said that, so is Happy Hardcore, so make of that what you will. Again, it comes in a variety of colours (sorry, *flavours*), all of which taste more or less the same. Smirnoff, of course, is the world famous Russian vodka, and they have successfully hitched themselves onto the alcopop bandwagon with **Smirnoff Ice** and **Smirnoff Black**. The general rule of thumb here is that Ice (cloudy) is for women and Black (clear) is for blokes. In fact, Smirnoff Black seems to be the only alcopop that is specifically marketed towards men, resulting, no doubt, in a Facebook explosion of identikit 'pub blokes' waving bottles of it around their stupid heads. Or possibly not.
RM

CARLSBERG

Carlsberg UK
Denmark, 3.8%

Brewed since 1904 and by appointment to no lesser establishment than the Danish Royal Court, Carlsberg Pilsner Beer is supposedly packed with the flavours of hops, grain, pine needles, summer apples and sorrel, whatever that is. Sounds like the perfect lubrication for the particularly Danish concept of cosiness and conviviality known as hygge (pronounced 'hooger'), which loosely translates as either, 'Brrr! Pint?' or, 'Sunshine! Fancy a couple of cans in the park?' depending on the season. Carlsberg, when brewed in its native country and to its traditional strength, could well be – as their bold as brass adverts claim – probably the best beer in the world. (Admittedly, for the travelling connoisseur, the first round of drinks in a Copenhagen alehouse usually costs about the same as the flight there from the UK, but we'll not dwell on that for longer than necessary.) The reality is, however, that the Carlsberg served in the pubs of Britain can be pretty much summed up by using one of the following words: piddle, widdle, wizz or wazz. Gone is the smooth malty dryness of the Danish recipe, and in its place a pale imitation, churned out by Tetley's, and weakened for the less refined palates and hair-trigger temperaments of the Brits to a pitiful 3.8%. Castrated, declawed and stripped to its underwear, the resulting brew is utterly indistinguishable from the insipid likes of Foster's or Carling or the contents of a dirty bucket left out in the rain. Now how the hell was that allowed to happen? *MJ*

CARLSBERG EXPORT
Carlsberg UK
Denmark, 5% ABV

Carlsberg in its Export variety is a premium strength lager still brewed according to the original Danish recipe with its deep malty notes generating a – not unpleasant – distinct bitterness. It was the first leading lager to be available in an extra cold incarnation, if you prefer your lager a few degrees under the norm. And it is now possible to enjoy Carlsberg Export on draught in your home, without going through all the rigmarole of converting your garage into a bar complete with proper pumps, wonky dartboard and sticky carpets. There exists in this world a device called the Carlsberg DraughtMaster which allows you to partake in pints of Carlsberg Export – with the ability to 'plug and pour'. And this from the company that also brings you Carlsberg Edge – a lemon and lime-flavoured beer. It's all certainly a long way from the rolling hills of Denmark back in the 19th century where Carlsberg was first created. JC Jacobsen was the brains behind it, and he began his career working as a brewer in a small brewery in the middle of Copenhagen, which just happened to belong to his father. However, JC soon got itchy feet (or whatever the equivalent that brewers get – needy hops?) and set up on his own, managing to find an idyllic spot for his own brewery in the hills of Valby, just outside of Copenhagen. To come up with a suitable name for the brand, he took the Danish word for hill, 'berg', and suffixed it with the name of his five-year-old son, Carl; hence: Carlsberg. *RM*

CARLSBERG SPECIAL BREW

Carlsberg UK
Denmark, 9% ABV

I could kick off this review with a mention of this lager's peppery spiciness or dry finish or even its foamy head, but there's only one real pertinent fact that you need to concern yourself with here and it's a big number 9. Yep, this stuff weighs in at a whopping 9% volume in the alcohol stakes, which puts it into the class of 'super strength' lagers and makes it a rather – how shall I put it? – acquired taste... The Danish rocket fuel was actually first brewed in 1950 to commemorate a visit to Copenhagen by Winston Churchill – a hero to Danes who had suffered so terribly during the Second World War. Now, it's well known that he liked a drink (Lady Astor: 'Sir, you're a drunk!' Churchill: 'Yes, Madam, I am; but in the morning, I will be sober and you will still be ugly!'), but even Winston must have winced when he first took a sip of this stuff. Apparently it contains cognac notes to reflect the great man's favourite tipple, but it's unlikely he got a chance to detect them, his palette more than likely completely slayed by the intense alcohol bite. These days it's pretty unlikely that many ex-Prime Ministers enjoy the merits of Special Brew (Tony Blair has yet to be photographed supping a tin), but it remains very much de rigour among that hardy band of folk who enjoy hanging around outside train stations. If Special Brew is too much for you, then you might try Carlsberg Elephant at a measly 7.2%. And if regular Carlsberg packs too much of a punch (ha!) try Carlsberg Mid Strength at 2.6%, or even Carlsberg Low Alcohol at 0.5%. *RM*

CASTLEMAINE XXXX

InBev
Australia, 3.7 – 4% ABV

In 1857, brothers Nicolas and Edward Fitzgerald (who came from Castlemaine in Ireland) rolled into town and built a brewery, and, in 1889, the Castlemaine Brewery was the first in Queensland to produce lager-style beers. Many years later we were told that 'Australians wouldn't give a XXXX for anything else.' How we laughed. How typical it was of those cheeky Aussies, and how much fun we had putting the f-word in place of the XXXX. Don't you just love catchy advertising gimmicks, eh? I suppose they had to compete with Crocodile Dundee doing the voice-over for another Australian lager, so with Foster's stereotyping all of their blokes as rugged bush-tucker-survivalists, Castlemaine categorised them as loveable rogues who would put drinking cool slabs of grog ahead of, well, everything including life itself. (We have those types in the UK, but seldom is the image so romantic and light-hearted.) In 2008, life imitated art as the news reported that some moron in the outback was pulled over in his car for having a crate of lager secured by a seatbelt while a five-year-old boy in the car did without. I'm sure there's another comedy ad hidden in there, if only they had the nerve. I'm not too sure why Australians, or anyone else for that matter, would risk life and limb for anything as mediocre as this. If you couldn't give a flying one about what you pour down your throat, then this is the one for you. Load of generic, tasteless, non-descript XXXX. *SW*

COBRA BEER

Cobra Beer Ltd
India, 5% ABV

Forget the fact that it's less Shilpa Shetty and more Jade Goody in origin, Cobra is a fine accompaniment to the UK's favourite food – the Indian curry. The perfect tipple with which to wash down a late night tikka masala, Cobra was founded in London in 1989 by 27-year-old Cambridge graduate Karan Bilimoria, who saw great potential for a lager that was less gassy, leaving the drinker less bloated and with more room for food. Already carrying £20,000 of debt, Bilimoria sourced a suitable brewer in Bangalore and, from his flat in Fulham, began to import beer and sell it to London restaurants from the back of a Citroen 2CV. The beer quickly became as hot as a vindaloo, and Bilimoria became a millionaire. Now brewed in deepest Bedfordshire, Cobra is billed as 'the UK's fastest growing world beer', and is sold in near-on 50 countries. The 'less gassy' factor doesn't spoil the taste. It's certainly not flat, more smooth, like all good lagers should be. It tastes clean, without any hint of harshness, and is deceptively strong. But there's no real 'kick' of alcohol in either the flavour or aroma, and the aforementioned 'smooth' factor means three or four pints go down nice and easy. There are alcohol-free and low-calorie versions lurking out there, as well as the genuinely interesting 8% King Cobra – a double-fermented lager served in a champagne-style bottle. And of course, it really does go down well with a nice madras. *DA*

COORS LIGHT

Coors
USA, 4.5% ABV

Burt Reynolds – the 1970s heartthrob and possessor of a monumentally hairy chest and an incredibly luxuriant moustache – once put his life on the line for Coors. Not literally, that would be ridiculous, but the plot of his classic film *Smokey and the Bandit* centred around the illegal transportation of cases of Coors across the US from the west coast to east coast. It sounds odd, but Coors was very much a regional product at the time and it really was illegal to ship it east of Texas due to arcane liquor laws regarding its brewing process, which involved filtering rather than pasteurising. Even further back in its timeline – the 1920s to be precise – Coors had to contend with prohibition in the US by diversifying into other products, including malted milk and – somewhat bizarrely – ceramics. (The ceramics company still operates today, fact fans, under the name CoorsTek.) Coors is legal across the US these days, and comes in Original and Light varieties. Here in the UK we only get the starch-reduced Coors Light, recently relaunched on these shores with a paltry £11 million marketing push. Taste-wise it's pretty inoffensive, with no real strong flavour and very little in the way of aftertaste, and, on the whole, it's not the best bottled lager I've ever supped. Let's put it this way; if it ever becomes illegal again you won't find me growing a moustache and leaping into a Trans Am to smuggle it anywhere in a hurry... *RM*

CORONA EXTRA

Wells & Young's
Mexico, 4.6% ABV

Light and refreshing, and served with a slice of lime in
the bottle neck, Mexican lager Corona is a suitably
pleasing summer tipple, effortlessly conjuring up images
of sombreros, mariachis, tacos, piñatas, illegal US border
crossings and Emiliano Zapata-style moustaches. 'Corona'
means 'crown' in Spanish – although labelled 'Corona
Extra', the 'Extra' bit is seldom used, or even noticed. But
what's with the lime? A pub bore might well try to
convince you that it is intended to keep away flies, or to
sanitise the bottle. Both explanations are myths. The
truth is down to Corona's clear glass bottle. Light makes
hops-derived compounds degrade, which is why beer is
traditionally stored in brown or green bottles. Clear
bottles are cheaper to produce, but beer stored in clear
bottles can produce a 'skunky thiol', which has a light but
musty smell. The lime was originally inserted to mask
the smell, and now adds a unique selling point to the
brand. From skunky to funky courtesy of a simple slice of
citrus. (Miller get around the 'skunky' problem in their
clear bottles by adding an extra compound to their
product – not nearly as interesting.) But what the hell is
a 'skunky thiol'? According to scientists at the University
of North Carolina, who someone paid real money to study
this question, it's an analogue of a compound found in
skunk glands. Suddenly that cold bottle of Corona doesn't
seem quite so refreshing. Ay, el estomago! *PB*

COURAGE DIRECTORS BITTER

Wells & Young's
UK, 4.8%ABV

Hold a pint of Directors up to the light and you'll notice that the colour of the beer matches the colour of the pump clip. There's no coincidence there, the dark ruby red hue comes from the use of roasted barley in the brewing process. Directors stands as a true stalwart in the real ale world of micro brews, themed beers and seasonal ales. It also happens to be the favourite beer of Steve Coogan's alter ego Alan 'A-ha' Partridge. Don't let that put you off though, first brewed by Courage in the late 1700s and now owned by Wells and Young's, this bitter really drinks easily. The 4.8% ABV delivers a fruity mouthful balanced with a strong hoppy finish. It goes down great with a Sunday lunch. The beer itself gets its name from the fact that the directors of the Courage brewery in Alton, Hampshire, used to reserve this brew for themselves as an in-house perk. Rumour has it that an employee sneaked a sample out to a local pub where it was greeted with great enthusiasm. The breweries directors were then persuaded to market it to the general public as Alton IPA. Locals knew what this new beer really was and called it Courage Directors, and eventually that name stuck. Well worth a try, if only to pay homage to Radio Norwich's finest DJ, and most definitely best enjoyed at the hotel bar of a Linton Travel Tavern. *GT*

DIAMOND WHITE

Gaymer Company
UK, 7.5% ABV

It's probably fair to say that a lot of people think the current vogue for drinking bottled cider in pubs (as opposed to drinking it on trains and outside of court) began only a year or two back when Magners/Bulmers brought us the cider-over-ice revolution. Not true: bottled cider Diamond White has been around since the 1980s, and was as synonymous with that decade as fingerless gloves or Anita Dobson's perm. At a hefty 7.5% ABV (which led some to christen it 'Diamond Fight'), the foolhardy even used this white cider as a basis for one of the more infamous 'cocktails' of the time – the 'Blasta-way'. This cheeky little number consisted of a bottle of Diamond White mixed together in a pint glass with a bottle of Castaway (a rather vile sparkling white wine and fruit juice combo) to produce a liquid which resembled tramp's urine. Such was the Blastaway's sharp taste that the first sip invariably drew your face into a rictus grin leaving you looking like Jack Nicolson's portrayal of the Joker in *Batman*. Diamond White was never the classiest of drinks (and it spawned an even tawdrier copycat beverage, White Lightning), but it has survived and is still available in cans and bottles today, although it's probably fair to say that it's now more popular with park bench residents than those looking for a cool and sophisticated tipple. *RM*

EFES

Efes Beverage Group
Turkey, 5% ABV

If you've ever been to Turkey, then you're certainly aware of Efes. The brand holds an 80 percent market share in its home country, so if you order a beer in Turkey there's an 80 percent chance you'll be served Efes. But there is no longer a need to travel to Turkey (and begrudgingly hand over your highly suspect £10 sterling 'entry fee' at the airport) to drink from the Efes fountain. It's now distributed around the world, and widely available in UK supermarkets. The Turks began brewing Efes Pilsner in 1969, and the Efes Beverage Group now owns 14 breweries. The secret to Efes' success? Bottom fermentation. Tee – and indeed – hee. That's actually the name of part of the brewing process, using malt, barley, and Hallertau hops. The result is a pleasant pilsner, easy to drink on holiday, soothes the pain of sunburn and mosquito bites, makes you forget which apartment you're staying in, helps you survive a bruising encounter with a moped on an unlit dirt track, perfectly accompanies the watching of a dodgy copy of a blockbuster movie on a sun-blanched bar telly... you get the idea. But should you be seeking it out back in Blighty? Would a Turkish tourist seek out Carling back in Istanbul? One thinks not. So what next for the mighty Efes corporation? That'll be 'Efes Dark Brown' in which, and I quote: 'the famous beer maker has successfully blended the flavours of the world's favourite cold and hot beverages – beer and coffee.' Roll up, roll up. Or, indeed, don't. *PB*

ERDINGER WEISSBIER

Erdinger Weissbrau
Germany, 5.3% ABV

The Bavarian town of Erding doesn't have many things to shout about. Right in the middle of Bavaria's high tech belt, known as the lederhosen and laptop zone, it's most interesting fact is that it is home to the world's largest wheat beer brewery. Erdinger is a top fermented beer, meaning the yeasts are active in warmer temperatures and begin acting on the brew as soon as they are added. It's also a wheat beer, which means more carbon dioxide, less hops, and – according to Erdinger – more refreshment. Germans are renowned for their beer purity laws, which for a long time meant only barley hops and water could be used in the brewing process. Amazingly, wheat was only added to the list of sanctioned beer purity law ingredients in 1987. Before that date, brewers had to apply to – and fatten the wallets of – local bigwigs for licences to brew these notoriously fruity and strong beers. So if it's a wheat beer, why is it referred to a weissbier, or white beer? Quite simply, and obviously, it's both. The Erdinger Weissbrau brewery is the biggest wheat beer producer in the world, but Erdinger Weissbier is a fairly ordinary example of the style. Its flavour is middle-of-the-road, and hardly bursting wheat beer fruitfulness, producing a mellow clove flavour, subtly tinged with banana, with a vanilla wheat aftertaste. It does, however, represent a decent introduction to the world of wheat beers, offering super refreshment and is worryingly easy to drink on a hot day. *GT*

FOSTER'S

Scottish & Newcastle
Australia, 4.0% ABV

Brewed in Reading, spiritual home of the kangaroo and institutionalised racism, the 'Amber Nectar' is as Australian as Mel Gibson, Andrew Symonds and good manners. But let's be honest, cobbers, this is essentially cooking lager, popular because it's widely available, generally cheap, you can go all day on the stuff without losing the ability to sit down, and, unlike its main in-pub adversary Carling, it hasn't become a byword for ironic haircuts, distressed jeans, casual violence, Kasabian listening, and general 'lads together' nonsense. So, despite Australia's carefully maintained reputation as the cultural dunny of the world, Foster's is relatively sophisticated compared to rival lagers. And, according to a man on the internet, we in the UK drink 30 pints of it a second (which possibly counts as binge drinking). The flavour is best described as 'inoffensive' and is dependent more on the potwasher's diligence and choice of soap than on vague abstract notions such as 'hops' and 'brewing', but then Foster's drinkers are unlikely to bother with tasting notes. Many pubs now offer 'premium' Foster's Super Chilled to the unwary and unthinking – essentially a freezing cold pint with an immovable 10mm of polystyrene foam on top and an effect on your innards roughly akin to that of battery acid. One TV advert for Super Chilled features the Violent Femmes song *Blister in the Sun*, which, as any alternative rock fan knows, is about excessive masturbation. What onanism has to do with Foster's is best left to the imagination, Bruce. *NS*

FOSTER'S TWIST

Scottish & Newcastle
Australia, 4.5% ABV

Ever get the feeling you've been cheated? Not so long ago, you couldn't get moved for cosmopolitan types swilling Corona with a slice of lime on sun terraces and beer gardens across the globe. (Admittedly it was always raining, but who lets the weather dictate whether or not they wear sunglasses on their heads these days?) Okay, it was essentially lager and lime, but it was *cool*. Now Foster's, chasing a cut of the Corona peso, have unleashed Foster's Twist – lager pre-loaded with a twist of citrus – upon an unsuspecting drinking world. This isn't *essentially* lager and lime, it bloody well *is* lager and lime, and as such it is very much *not cool*. Foster's have foolishly taken on Corona armed with a 'laid back lager' marketing campaign that claims Twist makes drinkers so laid back as to be almost horizontal. Surely all beers have this ability if taken in sufficient volumes – and others manage to do it while retaining some dignity. The only possible advantage Twist has over Corona is that there is no chance of it being served with that rotten lime segment that's been lying in a saucer behind the bar all day. I've selflessly taste-tested eight bottles of the stuff, but still can't work out what the point of it is. The word that best sums up Foster's Twist is: why? If you like lager and lime, by all means drink lager and lime – but please never do so in any boozer I am slumped in the corner of. *SG*

GAYMER'S OLDE ENGLISH

Constellation
UK, 4.5% ABV

Part of the Constellation group, the Gaymer Cider Company announced in March 2008 that is was giving Gaymer's Olde English Cider a £1.2 million marketing boost with a new 'contemporary' packaging design. That an 'Olde English' cider needs contemporary packaging must say something about current UK drinking trends. Gaymer believe that the updated packaging will bring new customers to the brand – which is more than the taste can be doing. That's the problem with Olde English: it looks bright and golden, and it sounds traditional and full of history, but unfortunately it doesn't quite work on the palate. Although it has been brewed under the Olde English name since the 18th century, its production was transferred to Shepton Mallet in Somerset in the mid 1990s after over 200 years of cider making in Attleborough in Norfolk. The brewers reckon they have been able to replicate Norfolk water in Somerset without affecting the taste, but can a drink really taste the same after its production is shifted across the country? One thing that has definitely changed is the ABV – reduced from 5.3% to 4.5%. What ye olde cyder drinkers would make of this is anyone's guess. Back when it was first brewed in the 1770s, farm workers were paid for their efforts with gallon-jugs of Olde English – perhaps the 18th century equivalent of minimum wage. Back in the 2000s, Gaymer has started sponsoring music festivals – and when you're up to your oxters in mud and music, who cares what you're drinking? *HC*

GAYMER'S ORIGINAL CIDER

Constellation
UK, 4.5% ABV

As inevitably mentioned elsewhere in these pages, the transformation in the image of cider has been quite remarkable in recent years. The addition of a few simple cubes of frozen water has elevated cider from being the choice of one stereotype to a drink enjoyed by another, possibly more annoying stereotype who – in the adverts, at least – look as if they'd sooner exclaim, 'Okay-yah!' than, 'Oo-ar!' Take Gaymer's Original, for instance. A £4million ad campaign featuring a series of bright young things enjoying life to the full made one thing very clear – this ain't Olde English. 'As good as it gets,' claimed the ads, a bold – some might say ludicrous – claim, but full marks for having confidence in their own product. Launched in 2006, the brand is marketed in a chic-but-dull premium bottle, perfect for supping in a faceless trendspot. A relatively new tipple from a very old company, Gaymer's Original is obviously produced by the Gaymer Cider Company – so, pedantry fans, why is there no possessive apostrophe on the new bottle logo if 'Gaymers' belongs to Gaymer? Gaymer still make cider using the traditional pressing methods that they have been using for centuries, and source English apples from their own orchards. Their bottles of Original are not as strong as some other ciders around, but it still tastes as any cider should and will no doubt always appeal to whichever stereotype the advertisers want money from. *RM*

GREENE KING ABBOT ALE

Greene King
UK, 5% ABV

One of the world's foremost writers on beer, Michael Jackson (no, not that one), has hailed Abbot Ale as being 'one of the great characters of the beer world'. Characters? I don't know if it's possible to imbue drinks with personalities ('Oh God, here comes that John Smiths, he's a right dour bugger'), but Abbot Ale certainly has some history behind it. It's brewed in the Suffolk town of Bury St Edmunds, where they've been at it for centuries. Indeed, you can trace brewing in the town back to 1086 (just twenty years after William the Conqueror first rolled up in England) when the 'cerevisiarii' (or ale brewers) were recorded going about their business in the Domesday Book, as servants of the Abbot of the Great Abbey of St Edmundsbury. Abbot Ale itself is brewed by Greene King, who have been making all their beers in the town since 1799. The brewery still draws water from the well sunk into Bury St Edmunds' chalk beds that the original beer makers used. Abbot Ale is Greene King's flagship brand and is brewed longer than many other beers, with pale crystal and amber malts giving it an attractive colour, a malty richness and a pleasingly bittersweet finish. Michael Jackson (no, still not that one) recently died, but I'm confident he'd still raise a glass to a pint of Abbot, along with many other ale drinkers who enjoy this quality cask tipple. *RM*

GREENE KING IPA

Greene King
UK, 3.6-5% ABV

Greene King call this is the UK's number one award-winning cask ale. Benjamin Greene, grandfather of *Brighton Rock* writer Graham Greene, established the Greene King's Westgate brewery in 1799, and India Pale Ale found its way to British drinkers via a shipwrecked cargo en route to India in 1827. If you're a seasoned lager man, then the chances are that you'll not like this because it isn't fizzy, and, well... it doesn't taste of lager either. I don't really know what 'a hoppy taste' actually tastes of, nor can I adequately describe it, but IPA certainly isn't unpleasant, and, like Brown Ale, I can neck a couple if they are freezing cold and not feel like I've been unfaithful to my beloved lager. It's not as dark as Brown Ale (paler, in fact), and being quite a strong one, you certainly do feel the effects while deciding whether you like it or not. I don't know if it is a cunning plan or not, but the bitter aftertaste made me thirsty and unable to stop drinking it; and not because I *want* more of it, either – just because I don't happen to have any lager in my fridge. I assume this is what's known as an acquired taste. As far as I see it, I don't want to taste anything bitter. Sweet is fine, even dry, but bitter to me is just wrong. Bitter is not enjoyable. But IPA has been around for yonks, so there must be plenty of people who like it. *SW*

GROLSCH

SABMiller

Netherlands, 5% ABV

Pop fans have been known to wear some downright ridiculous things in their time to show allegiance to their idols. Take Bay City Rollers nuts, for instance, who saw nothing odd in trimming their bell-bottoms with yards and yards of tartan. And then there were the Adam and the Ants aficionados who wouldn't cross the door unless done up like Captain Hook's disadvantaged brother. And then we have the Brosettes – an army of teen girls aligned to 1980s boyband Bros, a low-quality trio that somehow managed to crash the charts with tracks such as *When Will I Be Famous?* Brosettes had a strict dress code which involved puffa jackets, ripped jeans, Doc Marten boots and, curiously, Grolsch bottle tops tied to their bootlaces. Think of Grolsch and you immediately think of that bottle top – a stopper attached to the bottle neck that could be opened with a satisfying flip action, eliminating the need for a conventional bottle-opener. It is doubtful whether any Brosettes knew the rich history of the Dutch brewery – which was founded back in 1615 – but for me this premium lager definitely tastes better out of the bottle than on draught, although the bottle-drinking experience is undoubtedly enhanced by the pleasure that can be had in fiddling with that unique top. If you do decide to pop out for a Grolsch, why not try one of the various hostelries in the South London area? Chances are that one of Bros will actually be serving you.
RM

A Non-Beardy Guide to COCKTAILS

There remains a certain stigma attached to drinking cocktails that even the advent of the mixological age and the rise of über-cool identikit drinking holes has been unable to shake off (all irony intended). No self-respecting alpha-male would even consider striding into his local *Queen's Bodypart* and loudly ordering a **Fuzzy Navel** or a **Pina Colada**, or any of the brightly-coloured favourites that follow here. But cocktail bars are gradually usurping proper pubs, so let's start this round up with the cocktail that is often viewed as the acid-test of a bar – the **Mojito**. Perfected only in fables, but, made well, it's the stuff of legend, with the two warring flavours of the honey in the rum and the good fresh zing of the mint. Pretty much as pretentious as they come, but a very tasty touch none the less. Next up, we have the **Cosmopolitan**: cranberry, vodka, triple sec, lime – simple, but effective. A favourite with the fairer sex, but it would take a brave man to order anything that comes in an ostentatious Martini glass. Except, of course, for a **Martini** – both vodka and gin varieties feature in the top echelons of any cocktails guide: mixed, shaken, stirred – however you take it, just don't put on that ridiculous Bond-alike accent at the bar. You'll look like a prize wanker. Next up, arguably the top of the cocktail pops, the **Bloody Mary** – basically cold spicy soup in a glass, it kicks you in the back of the throat and is designed to be such an assault on your taste buds that any and all signs of hangover are swiftly forgotten. Everyone claims to have the definitive recipe, with the spice elements seemingly being interchangeable between Worcestershire or Tabasco sauce, Szechwan pepper, horseradish and multifarious others. This drink is single-handedly also making sure celery salt doesn't disappear off the culinary map – no, I don't know what it is either. That's the classier end of the cocktail list covered, now for the party drinks – recognisable for their zany, vaguely obscene names. Step forward **Screaming Orgasm** – a sickly-sweet, creamy (of course) mix of vodka, cacao, Baileys and silver top, and **Sex on the Beach** – a layered invention featuring Archers, vodka, cranberry juice and fresh orange, which is guaranteed to have any slack sally screaming outrageously at the barman's incredible lack of embarrassment. **Margaritas** tend to be a refined taste, and remain one of the simplest cocktails to make well (tequila, lime and sugar syrup in the right parts), but they can also have a worrying tendency to leave the drinker weeping in a ditch at 2am. And then there's the **Long Island Iced Tea**, a frankly devilish blend of gin, vodka, rum, tequila, triple sec, and mixers of coke, sugar syrup, lemon juice and sometimes egg whites. Again, it's one for the strong of stomach, as when it's made badly it takes on the same qualities and effects as turps, but when you find a good one, it's a keeper. *SG*

GUINNESS DRAUGHT / EXTRA COLD
Diageo
Ireland, 4.1% ABV

Ah, the black stuff; full of goodness and health, though
not wealth, the stuff of life, each pint a meal in itself,
each glass (half pint) the rumoured 'fix' for every malady
known to man. Made with water cascading from Wicklow
mountain springs, not the slow waters of the River Liffey,
Guinness pervades every corner of the globe. From the
old colonial pubs of the Sydney Rocks, to Manhattan's
ubiquitous 'Irish' bars, from the swish hotels of Hong
Kong, to the package tourist traps of the Med, this Irish
staple will likely be the first beer tap you see. My first
real Guinness session occurred during a 'business trip' to
Dublin that took three days to recover from, and I've
since become very partial to Guinness Draught, especially
when accompanied in the Irish style with a Jameson
chaser. But Extra Cold – served 3 degrees cooler than the
more traditional version – is now my preferred Guinness.
It takes 119.5 seconds to pour the perfect pint of Guinness Draught, apparently. Served in a two part pour, a
mix of nitrogen and carbon dioxide creates the alluring
Guinness swirl. Watch it tumble – a broth of muddy
brown slop, gradually clearing from the bottom, forming a
gloriously jet-black pint with a wonderfully creamy white
head, then savour the fresh coldness and the full stout
flavour with its traces of caramel and roasted hops. Most
definitely worth waiting for, so don't rush the barman.
WDL

GUINNESS ORIGINAL

Diageo
Ireland, 4.2 ABV

There's an old woman who sits with her dog in the snug of our local faux-Irish pub. She drinks Guinness, but swears blind that it tastes much better in Ireland. She also swears that her dog knows when it's his birthday. In short, she's bonkers. Nevertheless there remains a strong school of thought asserting that Guinness does indeed taste better in Ireland. Guinness itself has never put forward such notions. The official line is that, 'in blind tests (with a bunch of highly cynical journalists) none of our sample could tell the difference between Irish-brewed Guinness and the locally produced variety'. (What are they going to say: 'Yep – we keep all the best stuff for Ireland and flog off the rubbish to everyone else'?). Anyway, Guinness Original (and widget-fuelled Guinness Draught) comes in cans and bottles so, without the rigmarole involved in serving the draught variety, it should taste pretty much the same wherever you are in the world – and Guinness Original is a bottled delight. This is the stuff that is brewed to the original recipe which was first concocted by Arthur Guinness back in the 18th century when the ancestor of this beer was known as Guinness East and West India Porter. Think of it as the Guinness equivalent of a bottle of wine; strong tasting with a very distinctive roasted bitterness and an ideal accompaniment to a hearty meal – and, sod it, the ideal drink to actually make a meal with. It's just the job in a casserole. *RM*

GUINNESS RED

Diageo
Ireland, 4.1% ABV

Just what is it with all these new versions of popular classics? If you fancy a KitKat these days it's no longer a choice between two fingers or four. There's also KitKat Caramac, KitKat Dark, KitKat Chunky Original, KitKat Chunky Peanut Butter or KitKat Cappuccino to consider. And so it goes with Guinness. They already have Guinness Original, Guinness Draught and Guinness Extra Cold, not to mention various overseas varieties, and recently they've introduced a new draught onto the market, the 'smoother, sweeter' Guinness Red. Red? Surely one of the defining characteristics of Guinness is that it's black. Apparently you can't buy Red on the Emerald Isle, perhaps because tampering with an Irish classic to such an extent would be a travesty akin to renaming New Zealand's famous rugby side the All Reds. It still retains that creamy white head (a red and white Guinness should sell well in Sunderland, matching the football club's shirts and increasing appetite for all things Irish), and yes, it still does have a Guinness feel to it. The barley used to make the stuff hasn't been roasted to such a severe extent, meaning that while you still get that familiar roast bitter taste, it isn't as strong, leaving room for a subtle sweetness. And yes, you can still complete a cryptic crossword in the time it takes to pour, but it's not a bad tipple at all. As long as Guinness doesn't start bringing out Chunky Peanut Butter variations we'll not grumble too much. *RM*

HARP IRISH LAGER
Diageo
Ireland, 5%

Claiming to be Northern Ireland's number one lager, Harp was the first lager I ever tried; mainly because it was what the kind bloke who went to the offie for an underage me brought back. The advertising slogan of 'Harp stays sharp to the bottom of the glass' made it sound cool to drink, and when I first tried that warm, frothy, alien beverage it was my holy baptism into manhood. Or so I thought. The best thing about Harp (other than that slogan created by advertising maestro Rod Allen) was when they brought Irish Harp out in 1997 – again, with genius advertising. You could do a silly dance as you asked for a pint, laughing smugly like you were the first person to do so while the serving wench called you a rude word under her breath. Harp was a Guinness company product, bearing a Brian Boru Harp as its famous emblem until Diageo changed all that in 2005 when it separated the brand from Guinness and the Guinness-owned harp. So Harp doesn't even have a harp as a logo now. How rubbish is that? You have to go to Canada or USA to find a Harp lager with a harp on the side these days. They always ruin stuff. But not the taste... Harp has won six gold medals in the Monde Selection beer tasting competition, and is smooth, and, well... makes you want to drink more. And more. Which was my excuse the next day. *SW*

HEINEKEN

Heineken UK
Netherlands, 5% ABV

This perennial Dutch favourite has recently re-vamped its image. Heineken's previous incarnation on these shores was as a 3.2% ABV 'standard lager', a weakened version of its continental cousin brewed specifically for us puny Brits. Luckily those days are over, and drinkers are now treated to an imported brew with a vibrant and distinctively malty flavour, and a thirst-quenchingly good 5% ABV, which, after ten pints, can induce the ability to speak Dutch. As any visitor to Amsterdam will tell you, getting a bit of head is easy. Yes, for a few Euros you will be served a cold and quickly poured golden lager with a tight foamy topping. This head is vital to the overall enjoyment of Heineken; it adds texture and acts as a nice rule to see how fast you're drinking. Dutch barmen even have a tool to level the foam in your glass. This froth is so important to a glass of Heineken that the brewery employs a specialist to ensure that its famous white topping is kept 'ahead' of the game. This physicist has even had scientific papers published with titles such as 'The Role of Surface Viscosity in Gas Diffusion in Aqueous Foams'. A cracking read, that one. As far as rebranding goes, Heineken have done a top-notch job here, even going so far as to tilt the three letter e's in the label logo to make them 'smile' at you. So, if a trip to Amsterdam has left you with an embarrassing itch, remember that Heineken refreshes the parts other beers can't reach. *GT*

HOEGAARDEN

InBev
Belgium, 4.9% ABV

Although well known for its white beers since the Middle Ages, the Flemish town of Hoegaarden's last witbier brewery bit the dust in 1955. It wasn't until 1966 that the style was revived by, inevitably, a local milkman in, also inevitably, his hay loft. Nowadays, the idea of the stereotypical wacky Belgian brewing up a few barrels of intoxicating gloop for his mates has given way to mass production under the InBev umbrella. However, to this day Hoegaarden uses only the traditional ingredients of water, yeast, wheat, hops, coriander and dried Curaçao orange peel, which combine to give a taste a little like liquid Weetabix; and thanks to the heavily fibrous properties of the wheat, the beer resembles something along those lines when it comes out the other end the next morning. Commonly served with a slice of lemon or orange, for optimum enjoyment the manufacturers recommend drinking from a special Hoegaarden thick-sided, half-pint, hexagonal tumbler; the ton-weight Hoegaarden pint glass being a) far less common and b) a right bugger to steal without a sturdy wheelbarrow and a willing accomplice. And as well as causing heated discussions about its drinkability and take-that-back-ness over the years, Hoegaarden's pale, cloudy appearance and natural sediment has provided a perfect disguise for crumbs, floaters and caked-on fag ash for many an unscrupulous landlord. This cloudiness, to settle it once and for all, is thanks to an additional second fermentation in the bottle. So now you know. *MJ*

HOLSTEN PILS

Carlsberg UK
UK, 5.5% ABV

Probably the first of the 'designer' lagers, served in a small bottle that replaced Milk Stout and Barley Wine on the shelves and in the chiller cabinets of most boozers, the key to Holsten's initial success was its above-average strength, which prevented pint drinkers from calling you a puff for supping it. Then someone had the brilliant idea that Holsten could be marketed as a low calorie drink because all of the sugar had been turned to alcohol during the brewing process. However, drinking ten bottles of the stuff left you needing a 2000-calorie dose of kebab, so the Holsten Pils Diet died a swift death. But Holsten's sales still soared, largely due to a popular and imaginative advertising campaign featuring Jeff Goldblum playing his effortlessly smug, slightly spaced-out self. A sponsorship deal with Tottenham Hotspur followed and Holsten became a popular take home drink for armchair football supporters. Finally, we probably have Holsten Pils to thank for the disappearance of cholera and the black death. In the early days of bottled beer, it was often stored in cellars or pub yards where rats could piss on it with gay abandon. Since it was the habit of Holsten drinkers to eschew glasses, it meant every drink from the offending bottle was like a small inoculation against any condition that rats might pass on. Of course pubs take much more care with storage nowadays. Here's hoping, anyway. *MW*

JOHN SMITH'S EXTRA SMOOTH
Scottish & Newcastle
UK 3.8-4% ABV

In the world of ale drinking, frivolity is very much frowned upon. I know that, you know that and John Smith's know that, which is why they like to bill John Smith's as a 'no nonsense' beer. Even the name is a straight-up, honest-to-goodness, kind; one that is as English as a wet bank holiday and one that they hope we can do business with. However, despite its impressively non-frivolous merits, it's not a name that was chosen by a committee of market-testers, but is, in actual fact, the name of a real bloke. John Smith was born in Tadcaster, a market town in North Yorkshire. He began brewing his ale in 1847, and it swiftly won a hearty thumbs-up from the town's thirsty mill workers and factory hands. The company have maintained their down-to-earth image with a series of popular adverts, the most famous of which in recent times starred (tee-total) comedian Peter Kay. The classic ads saw Kay 'perfect bombing' his way to diving glory, spectacularly ruining a game of keepy-uppy ('Ave it!'), terrifying a young girl with tales of wardrobe monsters and burglars, and packing his 55-year-old mother off to an old people's home 'because I wanna put a snooker table in your bedroom and the kids are frightened of your moustache.' As it goes, John Smith's Extra Smooth is fairly innocuous, with the unadventurous taste, nevertheless, helping it to sell a million pints each day in the UK alone. *RM*

JOHN SMITH'S ORIGINAL BITTER
Scottish & Newcastle
UK 3.8-4% ABV

The majority of John Smith's sold in pubs and shops today is of the Extra Cold variety, but it is in fact Original Bitter that is the UK's bestselling real ale. How can that be? It's because Extra Smooth is pasteurised and filtered, and served from pressurised kegs rather than casks. According to beardier types than us (that's the folks at the Campaign for Real Ale (CAMRA)) only ales that are unpasteurised and unfiltered, and served from casks can be classed as 'real ales'. (CAMRA also accept bottle-conditioned ales, which are also unpasteurised and unfiltered.) So, despite John Smith's advertising direction favouring Extra Smooth, Original Bitter remains a huge UK seller as a solid, widely-available choice for the real ale drinker. It's an easy-to-drink session beer, perfect for supping on long afternoons down the Working Men's Club or old-school boozer. First brewed 160 years ago, John Smith's Original Bitter quickly became a Yorkshire legend – until S&N shifted production across the Pennines to Warrington. Yorkshire drinkers were furious, claiming that the Warrington-brewed version was flat and tasted odd. A boycott saw sales plummet and landlords returning full barrels. S&N admitted there had been 'quality issues', and shifted some production back to Tadcaster – but for how long? That story and the continued success of John Smith's Original Bitter goes to show that many drinkers know what they like and drink what they know. They like their no nonsense beer to be no nonsense. And you can keep your widgets, too. *PB*

KALIBER

Diageo
UK, 0.05% ABV

'Non-alcoholic beer? Pah! What's the point?' That's no doubt the review you were expecting, but, to be honest, I've got no real problem with non-alcoholic lager. It's a viable alternative for drivers, pregnant women, recovering alcoholics, and anyone who begrudges paying upwards of two bin lids for a carbonated cola. But I do have a problem with Kaliber. I'll admit this has nothing much to do with the drink itself, and everything to do with all those late 1980s TV ads featuring Billy bloody Connolly. 'Look at me! I'm Scottish and wacky! With a big beard that I sometimes dye blue! And I've got my willy out! *Again!*' When it comes to Billy Connolly, the word smug is wholly inadequate, and his infuriating ads were more than enough to merit a boot through the Rediffusion. '*I'm not a pheasant plucker, I'm a pheasant plucker's son, and I'm only plucking pheasants 'til the pheasant plucker comes.* And I've been drinking.' The ads, like Connolly, were bafflingly popular, and helped Kaliber survive in a difficult market, while the likes of 1980s non-alcoholic rival Barbican disappeared. It's brewed by Guinness as a full-strength, with the alcohol removed at the end. (Strictly speaking, Kaliber is not non-alcoholic as it does have a naturally occurring ABV of 0.05%.) Did I mention it's brewed by Guinness? Because that fact is writ large over Kaliber's packaging and advertising. 'It's brewed by Guinness! It's legitimate!' That may be, but I'm not sure I can ever forgive Kaliber for Billy plucking Connolly. And I've been drinking. *PB*

KINGFISHER
Shepherd Neame
India, 4.8% ABV

Kingfisher is the bestselling beer in India, and the UK's bestselling Indian beer, so far managing to hold off much-hyped newcomer Cobra. Indian friends of mine confirmed Kingfisher's popularity, but noted a difference in taste between the Indian original and the UK variety. That'll be because the UK variety is brewed in Faversham, Kent, by Shepherd Neame with yeast imported from India. While discussing the fact that the Bangalore brewery that created Kingfisher was founded by a Scotsman (Thomas Leishman founded the United Breweries in 1857), we enjoyed some home-made Indian pakoras and spring rolls. It's not always easy to find a beer that works with the spices of Indian food, but I dived into a bottle of Kingfisher and came out quite refreshed. It's brewed for a minimum of eight weeks, and comes in a very restaurant-friendly 660ml bottle. But is this a beer that should be drunk on any other occasion? My friends said they preferred the Indian brew, and certainly its UK cousin doesn't come close to competing with many of my favourites from Europe. It's light in colour and poured with a good head, but not much of an aroma. If anything, it was a bit sweet, and the taste – well, it was there one minute and gone the next, a bit like the bird it's named after, spotting fans. India is home to more than 70 species of kingfisher, and they are particularly prevalent around Bangalore. Interestingly, United Breweries also own one of India's biggest airlines – also called Kingfisher. *HC*

KOZEL
Plzeňský Prazdroj
Czech Republic, 4.8%

If Czech pilsner is the finest in the world, and those from the Plzeňský Prazdroj brewery the finest in the Czech Republic, then that brewery's Velkopopovický Kozel is arguably the finest of them all. From its 16th century beginnings in the small Czech town of Velké Popovice, this bitingly strong beer – perfect for people who like their beer to taste of beer with none of that fruity nonsense – finally acquired its Kozel name (meaning goat) and emblem in 1874, and has steadfastly resisted the vagaries of Bohemian history to this day, unless you count the baffling Axl Rose bandana on the goat that introduces the Kozel website. Unfortunately, Kozel is only available in bottles in the UK, so to enjoy it on draught you need to board a Stagnightair.com flight, take a rickety tram at least two stops away from the tourist masses, enter a dusty barroom and sit down at a table, place a beer mat in front of you and engross yourself in your Prague Post. Within five seconds – and without a single word being exchanged – a man with a battered waistcoat and a luxuriant moustache will stick a half-litre of Kozel on the mat. Drink it at your leisure. Blink. When you open your eyes, that same gentleman will have left you with another foaming glass and hot-footed it with your empty. This will continue until you work out how to stop him. And the bill for the whole lot will come to about a quid and a half. Including tip. *MJ*

KRONENBOURG 1664

Scottish & Newcastle
France, 5% ABV

The selling point of Kronenbourg lagers has for some time been geared around the better aspects of life enjoyed by our Gallic friends over the channel. A more relaxed, refined outlook. A little *laissez-faire*, perhaps. The composer leaving his work unfinished to enjoy a drink. The sexy French stunner, lager in hand, with the tagline that if you were looking at the advert in France, she'd not have her top on. All this sounds great, expect for the fact that the Kronenbourg 1664 you drink in Lyon is very different to the stuff you drink in Leeds. You've guessed it, it's weaker. 5.5% if you're in France, 5% in the UK. Why? Because we binge-drinking Brits can't handle full-strength lagers, perhaps, while the cafe-cultured French can sip the non-watered-down variety at their continental leisure? Okay, we're only talking 0.5% ABV here, but once again it's a bit of a kick in the teeth for UK drinkers, suggesting we're incapable of enjoying beer without getting hammered on the stuff. What we're left with is a fairly standard lager, from which the makers promise all sorts of things – notes of honey, aroma of grapefruit, a floral finish and even the taste of Mirabelle plum somewhere in the mix, whatever that is. Me, I found the whole experience to be typical of so many of the UK's bestselling lagers – it's cold and fizzy, but the taste isn't what it's cracked up to be, and that's a shame. *DA*

KRONENBOURG BLANC
Scottish & Newcastle
France, 5% ABV

An imported, fruity wheat beer from France which caused quite a splash when it landed in the UK a few years ago (possibly because of the astronomical costs associated with buying the stuff), Kronenbourg Blanc is a love it or hate it job, make no mistake. It's certainly fruity and quite refreshing, but it's sweet to the point of sickly, and you wouldn't want to drink more than a couple of pints of the stuff – although those couple of pints might be very enjoyable indeed. It's easily found on the high street and in the off-licence, and in my opinion that's no bad thing for UK drinkers who have suffered through years of nothing more than the mildest of mild ales and the blandest of bland lagers. The fact that many UK drinkers may very well turn their noses up at the acquired taste of Blanc is another matter entirely. It's also worth mentioning Kronenbourg Premier Cru here. Cru is a straightforward lager, albeit a 6% ABV one. The luxuriant bottle may be the most notable thing about it, as, for all its promises of quality, it doesn't really taste all that exceptional. The fact that it's advertised as an accompaniment to 'lobe de foie gras en consommé' (something I must admit to rarely having knocking around at the back of the fridge), shows exactly what type of market Kronenbourg are pitching Cru at. Good luck to the marketing team, hard luck to the consumers, and of course, their shrinking wallets. *DA*

LABATT BLUE

InBev
Canada, 5% ABV

If you find yourself with Canadian visitors who are
feeling a bit homesick, stick a moose head on the wall,
give them a hockey stick, and buy a case of Labatt Blue –
they'll soon be once again full of that Canuck joie de
vivre. Labatt is Canada's most famous and popular beer,
having got its foot in the door almost 160 years ago. It
used to be half-decent, too, but since being snapped up by
InBev its quality seems to have declined. It is still brewed
in Canada, apparently made with German aromatic hops,
yet there is hardly any aroma – or taste – worth mentioning. Back in the 1980s, Labatt's beer was sold to us Brits
by ads featuring Malcolm the Mountie ('he always gets
his can') played by Tony Slattery. Malcolm, with his
penchant for rescuing scantily-clad ladies from snow-
bound log cabins, was around for eight long years, before
being dropped after incurring the wrath of the real Royal
Canadian Mounted Police. Your bog-standard Labatt's
lager is now called Labatt Blue, and there's also Labatt
Ice if you're inclined to hunt it out. Regardless of brewing,
some will consider Labatt's biggest success was the
discovery of Pamela Anderson. The then-unknown Pam
was at a football game wearing a Labatt's T-shirt when
her image was shown on the stadium's screen, to the
delight of the crowd. She was invited down to the field,
and thereafter Labatt's offered her a modelling contract.
The rest of her career is, as they say, history. *HC*

LCL PILS
Thwaites
UK, 4.5-5% ABV

Good old LCL. More common a sight in North East working men's clubs than Gazza and Jimmy Five-Bellies out on a bender, LCL is always a staunch regular, and is almost as synonymous with Newcastle's drinking scene as Brown Ale. Now that's a bold statement, but LCL can hold its own in a one-on-one with any lager in town. Why? Because of its no frills, no nonsense approach to getting you off your head. Two more big plus points are that it's strong and cheap, making it a notorious way to spice up any meat draw on the planet. Born in 1997, LCL was bought by Scottish & Newcastle in 2004, as part of its acquisition of the Northern Clubs' Federation Brewery in Gateshead. At the end of 2007, S&N sold the entire rights for the production, marketing and sales of the LCL Pils beer brand to Daniel Thwaites Brewery in Blackburn. It didn't mean that the drink was destroyed or altered, and the chances are that the flat-cappers didn't notice or couldn't care less as long as it was still on tap. Its popularity lies in it being an honest pint. Why do you want a poseur's lager when drinking somewhere with no women to pull, and where you'll get your teeth kicked in if you ask for anything more elaborate than 'a pint'? It's also satisfying drinking a non-trendy name out of a bottle. It shows you know what you like, and LCL is an enjoyable lager without the pretentions of most others on the market. *SW*

LECH
SABMiller
Poland, 5.2% ABV

Of all the issues concerning immigration to the UK, Eastern European nations joining the EU, and the ensuing political fallout in this country, I think it's safe to say that one undeniably positive impact has been the widespread availability of various foreign lagers in your local boozer. Lech is such an example – and forgive the awful name for a second, because it's better than the draught rubbish we routinely drink. And the snappily-named Kompania Piwowarska (translated from the Polish it becomes the decidedly un-snappy 'Brewing Company') know they're onto something if the blurb on their website is to be believed. Talk about allusions of grandeur – they just plough straight with the claim that they make 'THE best lager in the world'. There is no 'probably' about it. I don't actually agree with their claim, but it's not the worst lager in the world either. Lech is quite bitter, and you'd ideally want it served very cold. And luckily, it isn't so strong it'll make you collapse, nor is it so weak you'll spend half your evening, afternoon, or morning (depending on your level of alcoholism) on the toilet. Available widely, it's not too hard to find in many of the major chain pubs, and you can also find it in cans and bottles at your off-licence or supermarket. The fact that it's not available here on draught at least means you'll never have the issue of a bad pint. Not a bad beer at all. *DA*

LEFFE BLONDE

InBev
Belgium, 6.6% ABV

I often have a glass of Leffe Blonde with a meal instead of wine, not least because it has its own attractive goblet glass, which is a *must*, although it's probably not for lager heads. As the name suggests, this is a light-coloured, almost amber beer, yet it has a wonderful deep, rich, caramelly flavour *and* has a great aftertaste, which is pretty rare in many of the beers I've experienced. I've noticed that almost everyone seems to have a different take on the flavours of Leffe Blonde – fruity or nutty or caramelly or whatever. This demonstrates that, like a great book, different people get different good things from a good beer. Watch out though – it's high in alcohol content, which may be a plus or a minus depending on where and when you're drinking it. It was originally brewed by monks in Belgium (hence it is known as an Abbey beer) and is still brewed to the same recipe in the town of Leuven, albeit now by the multinational corporation InBev. So it's one of a minority of brands owned by big corporations that hasn't been watered down for UK drinkers – yet. Dare I say this beer is good to cook with? That's both in the glass and in the recipe; it adds a sweet dimension to any meal. Admittedly, Belgium does produce better-tasting beers, but they are harder to find, especially outside of their native country. A final point – try not to mispronounce it – *Leff*, not *Leffy*! *HC*

LONDON PRIDE
Fuller's
UK, 4.7%

London Pride. What do those two words conjure in your head? If it's moustachioed men wearing plastic policemen's helmets and sporting feather boas, then your mind is clearly not on the job at hand. We're talking beer here, not gay pride marches. Now think *Cockney.* What is the image you get now? Is it a bull-necked 'geezer' propping up the bar of his local – taking time out from pontificating about all that is wrong with London (that it's full of moustachioed men in feather boas, perhaps) and barking his order for a pint of London Pride? Actually, scratch that image, too. Although I'm sure bigots enjoy it along with the rest of us, London Pride is decent bitter that, as the name suggests, can be found most readily in this nation's capital. It's the best known beer produced by Fuller's, a brewing company which was founded back in 1845, and has a pleasing mahogany colour and malty taste, which is balanced by three different kinds of hops. The firm is the last remaining traditional family brewer in London, and their historic Griffin Brewery in Chisick has the unusual accolade of being home to the oldest wisteria plant (a kind of climbing vine) in the UK. More plant connections? Well, *London Pride* is the title of a song penned by Noel Coward during the blitz in 1941, London Pride being the name of a plant which is noted for its ability to grow in even the most unfavourable urban spaces. So there you go. *RM*

LÖWENBRÄU

InBev
Germany, 5.2% ABV

Löwenbräu is a 'bottom fermenter'. Has that whetted your appetite for a drop? In fact all lagers are bottom fermenters; so called because they are brewed at much cooler temperatures than ales, at the bottom end of the scale (35-50 degrees Fahrenheit, rather than room temperature). They take longer to mature, but generally have 'less complicated' aromas than ales, and are often frowned upon by real ale drinkers. Löwenbräu, however, is a German lager, and the Germans know a thing or two about lagers. And Löwenbräu, in particular, has a real sense of history. The name, which – literally translated – means Lion's Brew, which can be traced back to 1383, when an innkeeper brewed his own beer at the 'Zum Löwenbräu' or Lion's Inn. 1383! That's 600-odd years of honing their brewing technique, and naturally they've got it down to a tee. I say 'naturally' and that's exactly how it is brewed, with all-natural ingredients. It's made according to the Bavarian Reinheitsgebot Purity Law, dating back to 1516, which states only the finest hops, barley, yeast and spring water may be used in the brewing process. The resultant drink is a very fine German lager, and a very fine German lager is well worth investigation. It is golden yellow in colour and produces a bright white head, and is particularly quaffable with food. Pub grub is okay, but it's best with sausages and sauerkraut at the Munich beer festival where bottom fermenter fans regularly raise a toast to it. *RM*

A Non-Beardy Guide to SPIRITS

In Scotland **whisky** is spelt without an 'e', everywhere else it's whiskey with an 'e'. Wherever, it's a minefield of snobbery – unless you are in your local back-street bar where your choice is likely to be between Jimmy No-Brand or Bell's. Your standard happy hour double or treble (with mixer) is Jimmy, while the good stuff is (supposedly) Bell's. You can apply this rule of thumb to every one of the main spirits, substituting Bell's for each other spirit, to burn your palette and corrode your stomach. Single-malt is regarded by puritans as superior to blended whiskey (made by mixing malt and grain whiskies), which, for argument's sake, is the Frankenstein's malt of whiskies. They are usually a bit cheaper too. The main differences between whiskies are by base product, alcoholic content and quality. Scotch is usually distilled twice, must be distilled in Scotland to be truly 'Scotch' and matured for at least three years in the cask. Irish is usually distilled three times and, according to law, must be aged in the cask no less than three years, but generally up to twelve years. Everyone is making it these days: Canada (usually Rye), America (Bourbon, Corn and Rye), Wales, Japan, India... even Russia, Germany and England are in on it. **Gin**, or 'mother's ruin' was invented in the Netherlands in the 17th century for 'medicinal purposes'. By the mid-1700s, gin became more popular than beer in the UK amongst the commoners as it was so much cheaper, but it built up a bad reputation as being the cause of social and medical problems.

Typical, eh? Best brands to look out for are Beefeater and Gordon's, closely followed by any generic London's Dry. If you think happy hour gin is bad, back in the early days it used to have turpentine and sulphuric acid added to it. My tip: Bombay Sapphire, tonic or lemonade, ice, slice of lime. Perfect. As the favoured cocktail staple of womanising fast car-driving James Bond, **vodka** is one of the world's biggest-selling spirits, with Smirnoff Red Label selling in excess of £220 million (said recent figures). Another white spirit, vodka's alcohol content varies much like any other, usually around 40% average. And again, buying an inferior brand of vodka can tend to leave you shaken and stirred. Your best bet is to look for a brand you recognise, because, like all generic non-branders, cheap vodka is as bad as buying non-brand breakfast cereal or DVD player. A notable climber up the vodka ladder is Glen Catrine's Glen's Vodka. **Rum**, usually drunk by pirates out of the bottle, originated in the Caribbean, where most of it is still produced. The drink became associated with the British Navy in 1655 when Jamaica was captured and French brandy rations were substituted for it. There are different grades; flavoured, light, white or silver, gold or amber, dark or black, over-proof and premium. It's only when you start investigating that you find out the similarities in production and public opinion. *SW*

LYNX PREMIUM
Booker
Netherlands, 5% ABV

Lynx is the UK's bestselling 'own-brand' lager, brewed in Holland exclusively for cash and carry wholesale chain Booker, and sold on through independent off-licences across the country. Unless you work in the trade, chances are you've never heard of Booker, despite the fact that they have 172 branches in the UK. But if your local offie has a 'Premier' sign above the door (and more than 20,000 UK offies do) then it's trading under a Booker brand. Lynx Premium is a 5% pilsner and, despite its 'value' price point and appearance, it punches above its weight when it comes to taste. Negotiating the minefield of own-brand lagers can be difficult, with many offerings being nothing more than cooking lagers, and others tasting suspiciously like re-packaged bigger brands. But supermarkets and wholesalers seem to be moving towards sourcing good quality premium exclusives that can compete with established brands. The increasing presence in the UK of value-based German supermarkets Aldi and Lidl and their solid own-brands has probably had an influence, and the UK big hitters have been swift to follow suit, like the mighty Tesco with its Boheme 1795 pilsner. Booker also produce a Lynx super strength – the 8.5% Lynx Altra – which is also a UK bestseller, outperforming the more established likes of Skol Super. Perhaps the thinking man's booze peddler, Booker instigated the literary Booker Prize for Fiction (now the Man Booker) in 1968. Now they receive the Non-Beardy Beer Book Prize for Best Own-Brand Beer. *PB*

MAGNERS ORIGINAL CIDER

Bulmers
Ireland, 4.5 ABV

Magners, Bulmers – whatever – it's all the same when it comes out the other end. Glaswegians were the first outside of Ireland to taste Magners, and with their seal of approval it must be worth getting hammered on. Eh, cider drinking is sociably acceptable? When did all this happen? Well, the secret of this pretention is the addition of the i-word. Ta daaaa... you no longer feel ashamed; you're sophisticated and fashionable. It tastes like apples, believe it or not. What else were you expecting? It is the perfect drink. Gorgeous. Everyone will bang on about drinking it in the summer, but I reckon it is a drink for any single day of the year. Picture a frosted pint glass loaded with ice cubes, a freshly opened bottle, the nectar fizzing down the bottle-neck as it's poured over the ice, cracking and bubbling all the way to the top. You're sitting outside in the height of summer, the sun beating down on your bronzed washboard stomach as your supermodel girlfriend brings the glass to your mouth. She runs her finger up the coldness of the glass then traces it over her lips before licking it. And then you wake up. You're alone in the house, no ice, a sad and uncultured pig, wincing at the harshness of the taste. You're watching the *Jeremy Kyle Show*, laughing. The sickly-sweet smell repeats on you as you burp, admiring the bottle, 'It looks just like Bulmers,' you say. *SW*

MARSTON'S PEDIGREE

Marston's
UK, 4.5% ABV

Marston's Pedigree is a very refreshing smooth pale ale, especially when served cool from the tap. With an ABV of 4.5% it may not be as strong as some run-of-the-mill beers like the wifebeating Stella Artois, but it packs a bigger punch than coming-of-age footy fans faves Carling or Foster's. I like how these old traditional brewing companies name their beers. As well as Pedigree, other beer names in the Marston's portfolio are Heart Warmer, Evening Glow and Ugly Sisters, which after a few pints you could rename the Not-So-Ugly Sisters. Marston's brewery was founded by John Marston in 1834 in Burton-on-Trent, and uses the famous Burton spring water in its ales. While most beers nowadays are brewed in stainless steel vats, Marston's brew their beers in traditional oak casks, linked together by pipes and troughs. Personally I couldn't care less if it was brewed in old Mrs Miggins's tin bath as long as it keeps tasting this good. Marston's Pedigree is also available to the home drinker in 500ml cans and bottles which I now stock up on a regular basis. No, I don't have a drink problem... yet. So, previously a Guinness drinker, I now feel I have found my perfect pint. So for a change from the norm, next time you're in a pub ask for a pint of Marston's Pedigree and tell them I sent you. They won't have a clue who you're talking about. *DL*

MCEWAN'S BEST SCOTCH

Scottish & Newcastle
UK, 3.6% ABV

A Scottish & Newcastle staple for as long as anyone can remember, the good old McEwan's Best Scotch pump was a bar top necessity across the North East of England well before the onset of drinking as a fashionable pastime. But getting the young punters in meant getting the old ones out, and nowadays McEwan's Best Scotch has been relegated to grubby granddad bars and working men's clubs. Southerners know Northerners like a drink, but are still shocked when they overhear them asking for 'a pint of Scotch'. But huge whiskies are not the order of the day – in fact Scotch refers to the method of brewing that gives this beer a very dark chestnut hue. It is generally served with an inch-thick head of foam – easy drinking and malty, with a peaty blandness, the old folks still lap it up. Billed as 'the one you've got to come back for' during a long ad campaign in the 70s and 80s; one of the TV commercials depicted a just-returned, homesick Geordie supping a pint of Scotch in his local, regaling misadventures at the Munich beer festival with flashbacks of clinking beer steins, lederhosen-clad men slapping each other. When asked by his local barmaid what the women were like, he simply replied, 'Ahhh man, giz a bag o' crisps!' It's a real shame; time is running out for this brew, its aging customer base will disappear within a generation and with them the legend that blokes up North sup whiskey by the pint. *GT*

MCEWAN'S EXPORT ALE

Scottish & Newcastle
UK, 4.5% ABV

One of Scotland's finest, this dark, caramelised beer promises 'quality and strength' and – like Ronseal – it does exactly what it says on the tin. Before ecstasy and the spliff, the four-pack of McEwan's was the ticket into any party you weren't invited to. Throw in a half-bottle of Glenmorangie and you'd be guaranteed first shot at the Twiglets and the choice of bedroom at any party in the land. Export is still sold on draught in many nicotine-stained bars across the country – any pub needing a makeover or with *Blanket on the Ground* still on the jukebox will probably serve a damn good pint of it. At 4.5% strength, it can hold its head up in most company. It is the beer of choice for many rail-travelling football fans, and is always prominent on a Friday on the East Coast mainline between Aberdeen and King's Cross – when anywhere up to 48 cans may be found on a table of four returning oil rig workers. Obviously the brew never makes the drinker abusive to ticket collectors, and it does so much to enliven and cheer up the quiet coach on long-haul journeys. Most travelling drinkers bring their Export onto the train in a carrier bag – in the supermarket it is an inexpensive buy, but on the railways it is more expensive to buy than a three bedroom terrace house in Leith. Proudly 'only ever made in Edinburgh, Scotland', McEwan's Export is a national treasure – it cannot be long before there is a GCSE module studying its history. *MW*

MERRYDOWN

Merrydown
UK, 7.5%

In the late 60s the cider industry was all but dead. Only a handful of Cornish thatchers and a few dozen morris dancers bothered with it and even then only if it had bits of wood floating in it. Beer was king. Then along came a marketing man who decided to make it a niche drink by sticking 'Vintage' on the bottle. Soon we were all buying it, hunting out a '68 in the belief that it was better than the '74. Fools that we were. Of course people still drank QC sherry or Mateus Rose at about the same price per bottle, and the Mateus bottle had the advantage of making a better lamp base than the bottle from Somerset. What Merrydown did successfully was gently introduce women to cider drinking, although, given current statistics on female binge drinking, this might not be anything to brag about. Today Merrydown represents the golden age of cider, when it was still happily made from apples grown lovingly in the orchards of the south west. It was the time before cider bottles came to be wrapped in plain brown bags, and the time before cider became chemically synthesised in a laboratory in Saffron Walden with 0% apple content and well before you'd use it as an image accessory to go with your boy band haircut. Now Merrydown is rehabilitated as a drink sitting happily on the shelves of Waitrose, a product with 40 years of tradition, unlike your alcopops and WKDs. *MW*

MICHELOB ULTRA

Anheuser-Busch
USA, 4.2% ABV

Picture the scene – an industrial American town under a big greying sky, where men are big and women are bigger, where industry is in the blood, and graft is the marker of a true man. Now ask yourself – what do these honest, wife-fearing, hard-working men drink when they knock off for home? Quite possibly Michelob Ultra, a beer that conjures up images of Minnesota millworkers and loggers and others of suitably gritty professions enjoying a hard-earned after-work tipple. I am but a humble British shop keep, and when I wish to feel manly, there's nothing quite as testosterone-nurturing as the pleasant metallic note of this vastly superior cousin of Budweiser. Be warned however, it tends only to be sold in places that feel the need to charge you a price that reflects every step of the brewing process. Michelob Ultra is an unpolished gem, rough yet smooth, and undeniably soulful, a true contender, if it were given half the marketing focus afforded to stable-mate Bud. It was invented by An-heuser-Busch co-founder Adolphus Busch in Fergus Falls, Minnesota in 1896. Ultra is the Michelob of choice for the UK, but US drinkers get a portfolio of Michelob beers ranging from the low calorie alternative to a gag-inspiring Pumpkin Spice Ale, presumably produced in some gaudy brewery version of Wonka's Chocolate Factory, where some buffoon is adding all manner of crazy ingredients to a vat of glorious Ultra. 'Mmm, pumpkin..! I think that's just zany enough! Hang the flavour consequences.' *SG*

MILLER GENUINE DRAFT
Miller Brands
USA, 4.7

Miller Genuine Draft, a 4.7% bottled beer, is not to be confused with Miller Beer, a 4.2% draught beer. So Miller Genuine Draft is bottled, and Miller Beer is draught. Crystal clear, right? Just like the long-necked bottles MGD is served in. The Miller Brewing Company is based in Milwaukee, famous for beer, Harley-Davidson and *Happy Days*. (A bronze statue of Arthur Fonzarelli is to be built on the city's Riverwalk.) Utilising the handy beer knowledge of thousands of predominantly German 19th century immigrants, Milwaukee was once home to four of the world's biggest brewers – Blatz, Pabst, Schlitz and Miller. Only Miller remains. Sometimes known as Brew City, Milwaukee of course has a baseball team called the Brewers that plays at Miller Park. The UK's favourite Miller brand, MGD is cold-filtered, which essentially means it isn't pasteurised with heat. But forget the taste, the real USP offered by MGD is its new twist-off cap. 'Purveyors of the uniquely cold filtered beer will find themselves one swift twist away from refreshment!' said Miller's marketing manager, announcing that further exciting developments would follow. 'The introduction of the twist-off bottles is just the start!' Man alive, whatever next? The bottle of beer that purchases itself, walks home from the off-licence, collects your takeaway, indulges in pointless chit-chat with the wife, turns on the telly, plumps up the cushions, and then pours itself down your bone-idle throat? Now *that's* a beer I'd like to get acquainted with. *PB*

MORETTI
Heineken UK
Italy, 4.6% ABV

Moretti is from Italy of course: it's Sophia Loren; it's Dolce & Gabbana; it's Gregory Peck and Audrey Hepburn gliding through the streets of Rome on a Vespa... it's all of these things and more – things that make the country the planet's capital of chic. But if this is the case then why oh why does one of Italy's leading beers picture a man who for all the world looks like an extra from *Heidi* on the front of its bottles? There he is, all Bavarian hat and bristling moustache, looking like he's more concerned about his goat herd than la dolce vita. As ever, though, there's a story behind it. Moretti was first brewed in 1859 by Luigi Moretti in a small quiet town in Northern Italy. It wasn't until 1942, however, that the character depicted on the label first arrived on the scene, when a descendent of Luigi, Leo Menazi Moretti, spotted a moustachioed old man sitting at a table in a local restaurant. Leo believed that the old gentlemen embodied the character and personality of the actual beer – genuine, traditional and authentic – and took a photograph of him. The image was retouched in colour and has since been used on millions of bottles of Moretti. The old man's payment? 'A glass of what I am drinking is sufficient for me,' he told Moretti (in Italian, presumably). The beer itself has won count-less awards (it recently claimed the gold medal at the Brewers Association World Beer Cup) and is a wonder-fully light and charming drink. *RM*

MURPHY'S IRISH STOUT

InBev
Ireland, 4% ABV

In the style of *Family Fortunes* we asked 100 people to name an Irish drink and the top answer was..? Yep, when you think of Ireland and you think of booze the first thing that invariably comes to mind is the black and white behemoth that is *Guinness*. Any other Irish drink has to stand in its immense shadow and is consigned to finish second, at best, in any popularity poll (or be content to play Buzz Aldrin to Guinness's Neil Armstrong, if you will). That said, Murphy's is a drink that has managed to carve its own niche amongst stout drinkers, and is now sold in over 40 countries around the world. And it's no Johnny-come-lately either, as it was first brewed in Ireland back in 1856 with the Murphy Brewery recently celebrating 150 years in the business of serving up the foamy stuff. But just how does Murphy's square up against Guinness? Well, many would attest to the fact that it is has a nuttier flavour than its more famous counterpart and that it also has a slight hint of coffee. There's also a matter of the aftertaste which isn't as bitter as you'll find with Guinness, something which the brand have played on with their 'Like the Murphy's, I'm not bitter' advertising campaign, which has certainly paid dividends in getting the drink noticed, especially in the US. The bottom line is: it's not Guinness, but it's not bad. *RM*

NEWCASTLE BROWN ALE

Scottish & Newcastle
UK, 4.7% ABV

The last true bottle of Newcastle Brown Ale was brewed in April 2005, after which S&N's Tyne brewery was closed and demolished. So Newcastle Brown Ale is now brewed across the River Tyne in Gateshead, at the Federation Brewery. Unsurprisingly, this has caused something of a hubbub on Tyneside, with Brown Ale as quintessentially Geordie as stottie cakes, pease pudding and Alan Shearer. The situation was not helped when an S&N spokesman ill-advisedly said, 'Most people think Newcastle and Gateshead are the same place anyway.' The European Union didn't agree, cancelling Brown Ale's precious Protected Geographical Indication status. Indeed, having already closed their Edinburgh brewery, the closure of the Newcastle plant saw cynics begin to refer to 'Scottish & Newcastle' simply as '&'. But such geographical disputes will hardly matter to Brown Ale's legion of fans outside of Geordieland. Known in some parts as 'Newkie Brown', and in the US simply as 'Newcastle', Brown Ale is one of the world's most famous and bestselling beers. Created by Colonel Jim Porter in 1925, Brown Ale quickly found favour, winning four gold medals at the 1928 International Brewers' Exhibition. The medals were incorporated into a commemorative label design, which remains pretty much unchanged some 90 years later. The label's famous five-pointed blue star refers to the five brewers who came together to form Newcastle Breweries. 'Broon' Ale is also known as 'Dog' in its city of origin, as in, 'I'm off to see a man about a...' *PB*

NEWCASTLE EXHIBITION ALE

Scottish & Newcastle
UK, 3.8% ABV

There is an old football chant that was popular among the rougher elements of travelling Newcastle United fans back in the 1980s. These fans would turn up en mass at various away grounds – nowhere flash given Newcastle's lack of success during that decade – and the chant would invariably rise up: '*We drink Ex, we drink Brown, now we're going to smash your town.*' Not the most endearing of ditties, certainly, and to be fair not many towns were smashed up, but plenty of Ex and Brown was undoubtedly supped; Brown being, of course, Newcastle Brown Ale, and Ex being Newcastle Exhibition. Both beers are brewed by Scottish & Newcastle, but while Newcastle Brown Ale has a mythology swirling around it and is sold all over the world, Newcastle Exhibition has always been something of a little brother (despite having an interesting history of its own, having first been brewed in 1887 to celebrate Queen Victoria's Diamond Jubilee). Exhibition was given quite a marketing push by S&N a few years back (via a series of TV ads that ended with a woman proclaiming, 'Ex, Ex, Ex – that's all you men think about!') but these days the beer is mostly enjoyed by those who've stuck with it over a period of time through thick and thin. These stalwarts can now only enjoy the beer on draught (cans of Exhibition were discontinued a few years ago), and their loyalty is rewarded with a very decent ale which has a pleasant maple aroma and aftertaste. And hopefully it won't make them want to smash up any towns. *RM*

OLD SPECKLED HEN

Greene King
UK, 3.8% ABV

There must be some kind of unwritten law that brewers adhere to which states that the more ridiculous the name of an ale, the better – or more authentic – they'll hope we'll think it is. You get the feeling that most of these daft names have just been dreamt up at the fag-end of various beer festivals ('Yeah, we'll call it Crusty Nun – sounds like a winner.') but some of them do have a genuine reason for being called something daft. A case in point is Old Speckled Hen, a name which doesn't actually have anything to do with farmyards or indeed hens. The ale was first brewed to commemorate the 50th anniversary of the MG car factory in Abingdon, Oxfordshire. The factory used an old MG car as a sort of run-around, and over time, this unusual, canvas-covered saloon became covered with flecks of paint and the locals began referring to it as the 'old speckled 'un', which gradually mutated into the 'old speckled hen', and thus a (admittedly parochial) legend was born. The beer is available by cask or in bottles (it's the number one choice at check-outs for those hankering after premium bottled ale) and its popularity is no doubt helped by the fact that the drink is a finely-balanced pale ale with a subtle blend of flavours. Apparently the brewers – Morland – use a unique strain of yeast first used in 1896, predating even the 'old speckled 'un'. (The MG factory, inevitably, closed in 1980.) *RM*

ORANJEBOOM
Shepherd Neame
Holland 4.1% ABV

It's claimed that Oranjeboom (that's *Oran-ye-boam*) has been around since 1671, although the beer hardly boasts a proud heritage. While blessed with a majestic concept – Oranjeboom literally translates as 'Orange Tree', symbolising the royal family tree of William of Orange – it is often regarded as the runt of the Dutch beer litter, behind Heineken and Amstel. Indeed, a bar sporting a big Oranjeboom sign is usually a dump, and a good place to see the extremes of the Dutch national characteristic of warmth and congeniality towards foreigners, mixed with utter hatred of each other. Evidence? Count the team-wrecking squabbles that have seen a premature exit from every World Cup and Euro tournament since year dot. In 1973, Oranjeboom suffered the ultimate indignity of being replaced by the Skol brand, which, while being unrelated to the economy lager of the same name brewed today by Carlsberg-Tetley, was still a regal kick in the goolies. As in other countries, however, the Skol name ensured mocking laughter and commercial failure, and the Oranjeboom name was restored in 1982. So how does it taste? Whether it's the 5% Dutch Dommelsche Bier-brouwerij original or the 4.1% British version brewed under licence by Shepherd Neame, Oranjeboom is not unpleasant, just a bit bland. Experts point to a cardboard box nose, a sweet hoppy taste and a metallic finish, which is just an elaborate way of saying that it's completely indistinguishable from any old mass-market swill. It's good with curry, though. *MJ*

PEETERMAN ARTOIS

InBev
Belgium, 4% ABV

Although it may be relatively new to these shores,
Peeterman Artois, named after St Peeter, the patron
saint of Leuven, was first brewed in 1794 as the original
flagship beer of the Artois Brewery. It was discontinued
in the 1950s, but then revived in the UK in late 2006 as a
light premium beer made from wheat, barley, malt and
coriander (although I'm not so sure coriander has ever
been an ingredient particularly demanded by beer
drinkers). It has a lower ABV than Stella, and has
perhaps been introduced as a response to Stella's
unfortunate association with alcoholic aggression. At a
sensible 4%, Peeterman should hopefully avoid Stella's
fate of being bestowed with a notorious spouse-abusing
nickname. A posh bar font and classy stemmed glasses
will no doubt help Peeterman satisfy the more upmarket
drinker. Brasserie Artois had previously introduced
Artois Bock to the UK at a hefty 6.2%, and they also brew
Stella Artois NA (biere sans alcohol), so the Artois family
now caters for a broad range of alcoholic needs. Peeterman itself turns out to be an undemanding beer in all
areas, light to the point of watery, not particularly
unpleasant, but just rather boring. It's obviously an
Artois response to Beck's Vier, another 4% variety of a
leading brand, and there is a suspicion that the big
brewers are seeking to capitalise on the UK's longer
drinking hours and weakness for binge drinking. Con-
taining 23% less alcohol than Stella, Peeterman is a beer
they want you to buy one more of. *HC*

PERONI NASTRO AZZURRO

SABMiller

Italy, 5.1%

There is something unerringly addictive about Peroni's 'blue ribbon' bottled lager, and it is not all to do with the taste. As you stand poised at the bar of a traditional Italian watering hole – because of course there is no better way to sup at 'Italy's finest' – and the first mouthful sparkles on the tongue you might wonder what all the fuss is about, which calls for an immediate examination of the bottle; herein lies the charm. In true Italian nature, everything about a bottle of Peroni, from its requisite royal blue, white and crimson red label brought to life against the green bottle, to its fitted, sleek design like a classic cut suit, is fashionable and instils a sense of opulence in its temporary owner and 'brings out the Italian in you'. The packaging design, by Brand Union, was themed 'effortless Italian style'. Peroni even showed their arrogance, I mean nous, for style for a brief time during the 2006 World Cup when classic shots of Italy's starting 11s from various International tournaments hugged the bottles – arguably the most retro wallpaper on a bottled beer ever. The bottle is so good, you'd be crazy to order a pint of the stuff, even if it probably does taste better from draught. Who would have thought drinking a certain type of beer would be a statement of style? And its style has brought success – Nastro Azzurro was the UK's fastest growing beer brand in 2007. Interestingly, the Italians themselves prefer Peroni Red, a 4.7% ABV bestseller in its home country. *JW*

A Non-Beardy Guide to WINE

Red or white, sometimes fizzy, comes from grapes. If you're looking for anything much more insightful than that about the weird wide world of wine then I'm here to tell you that you've bought the wrong book. The fact is you don't need to be Oz Clarke or Jilly Goolden to enjoy wine – I'm reliably informed that 75 percent of the UK's population drink it regularly, and, for the vast majority of them, wine is something to be drunk and enjoyed rather than pontificated about. As is our want, Brits shop by brand and price, and our wine market is dominated by a number of big hitters that each produce a reliable and affordable (some might say predictable) range of reds, whites and rosés. Britain's bestselling wines are mostly all mid-priced £5-10 brand names, and that means we tend to shun France and the rest of poncey old Europe in favour of the fresh and exciting New World. The UK's list of favourite wine brands is dominated by Australian tipples – a quarter of all wines bought in the UK now come from Oz (the country, not the ruddy-cheeked plonk expert). **Hardys**, **Wolf Blass**, **Lindemans**, **Jacob's Creek** and **Banrock Station** are all solid performers that offer wines unlikely to offend anyone's palate. Hardys is Australia's biggest player, while Jacob's Creek is probably the most respected of the mass-market Aussie brands. The US, and California, provides the UK's other bestsellers, from **Gallo**, **Echo Falls** and **Blossom Hill**. Gallo Family Vineyards is the UK's favourite US brand, and the E & J Gallo Winery, in Modesto, California, is the largest family-owned winery in the world. South African **Kumala** is another big New World seller. Looking further afield, **Stowells** offer a range of wines from around the world under their brand name, while **JP Chenet** is the UK's most popular French vino. But what about those pesky grape varieties? I have neither the time, inclination, or – let's be honest here – know-how to get into complexities, but here's an incredibly basic and wholly inadequate starter's guide: red Cabernet Sauvignon and white Chardonnay are full-bodied and good with food; red Merlot and white Sauvignon Blanc are fruity and great to drink on their own; red Pinot Noir is a classier (and more expensive) option, and red Shiraz is rich and spicy; white Reisling and Chenin Blanc are refreshing everyday wines; fruity and popular White Zinfandel is a posh rosé. That might not help much if you're struggling to choose a bottle for an important dinner party, but by sticking to a reliable brand you won't go very far wrong. And, while wine snobs might frown upon screwcap bottles, they're easier to open *and* eliminate the risk of 'corking'. Gotta love the screwcaps. So that's wine for you. Try it, buy it, drink it, and enjoy it. Explore and learn, if you're so inclined. You might well get a new hobby out of it. I'm sure it's all very fascinating – just don't come boring my ears about it, alright? *PB*

PILSNER URQUELL
SABMiller
Czech Republic, 4.4% ABV

Another claimant to being the original pilsner beer, Pilsner Urquell (that's ur-*kwell*, pronunciation fans) was first brewed in 1842 in Pilsen – the Czech town from which the name pilsner derives – by Josef Groll, a man so admirably bad-tempered he was described as the 'coarsest man in the whole of Bavaria'. As Bob Dylan is to every yowling busker, this is the stuff that every two-bob placebo lager is trying to emulate. And, being 160-odd years old, Urquell have had plenty of time to impose stipulations that would make the taxman blush. First of all, they demand Pilsner Urquell should never be consumed straight from the bottle, as you won't release the full crisp flavour or floral aroma. So get a glass. Next, rinse that glass with cold water for at least five seconds to get it to 7°C with a maximum variance of plus or minus 1°C, and then, using a protractor and some very patient friends, hold the bottle at a 45° angle and the glass almost horizontally. Now pour, if you can still be bothered. Be careful, though, as interrupted pouring can cause what they describe as a beer with a 'bald spot' and a 'cauliflower' head, or what the layman would call a pint that looks like Lawrence Dallaglio after a nine-try hammering. It's a damn fine beer, but, Lord, what a carry on. Is it any wonder that the fuss-free imitators have nipped in and pinched their market? *MJ*

RED STRIPE

Diageo
Jamaica, 4.7-5%

This was always the coolest, trendiest lager in the mid-late 80s. You couldn't go out in town without seeing groups of wannabe yuppie lads who styled themselves on *Diamond Lights* crooners Hoddle and Waddle: baggy suits with sleeves rolled up, thin leather tie, dodgy mullet haircut and a can of Red Stripe in hand, looking to impress the ladies. Those were the days, eh? A few years on from there and the bubble seemed to burst. It was no longer a drink for the fashion-conscious; they'd got their hair cut and moved on. But now it appears to be clawing its way back up – ever so slightly. I doubt it'll ever be as popular, but with its retro throw-back feel, I'm not too ashamed to neck the odd four pack (albeit in the house where no one can laugh at me). Red Stripe is strong and just about credible enough to drink in public and can still hold its own as an above average bevvy. Just like every beer or lager – it goes down a treat when cold and tastes, well... lagery. It's quite light tasting for a strong lager and is great to bring back those memories of trying to look rich and older than 17, but failing at both. Everyone will always mention the fact that it's from Jamaica when you drink it. They can't help themselves. It's as boring as 'swans can break your arm.' Just reply with 'Hoddle and Waddle reached number 12 with *Diamond Lights*.' *SW*

SAMUEL ADAMS

Shepherd Neame
USA, 4.8% ABV

If you've ever been in a bar in the US and fancied something other than the omnipresent Bud or Miller then you might well have settled for a Sam Adams. Now available by the bottle in the UK, tasting this sweet, amber beer with its malty overtones could bring back transatlantic memories. You'll remember humid Manhattan evenings, glorious Florida sunsets, and, most clearly, the fact that the Yanks still cannot make a decent mass-produced beer. At 4.5% ABV, Samuel Adams markets itself as a Boston Lager, yet upon first taste most people still think 'fizzy real ale'. Roasted malt gives a darker hue to the brew which imparts a deeper, more robust flavour yet it still remains easy drinking, at least when on draught, although it's overly gassy in its bottled guise. The labelling, with its old-style script and painting of Sam himself dressed in his 1770s poplin tunic, may sway you into thinking this Massachusetts brew has been around for generations. In fact, the beer was first brewed in 1984. Samuel Adams the man was a well known Bostonian, a pro-independence firebrand; he has been tagged 'the Father of the American Revolution', a true hero of American history. He did inherit a brewery from his father, so there is a link there, but the brewery went bust under his mis-management in 1764. So raise a glass of Samuel Adams to Samuel Adams the failed brewer but successful patriot, without whom there would be no Fourth of July! *GT*

SAN MIGUEL

Scottish & Newcastle
Spain, 5% ABV

Many folks' first encounter with San Miguel was on the Spanish Costas, where this cerveza has rendered many a package holidaymaker incapable of finding their way back to their self-catering apartment. Now a major brand outside of Spain, San Miguel has become popular in bottles and cans in the UK, and has recently become a common sight on draught. Initially marketed as a premium lager at a premium price, San Miguel's original strength of 5.4% ABV meant that it was sometimes tagged with the non-PC nickname 'senorita beater'. Drink awareness campaigns and taxation issues have meant the UK-brewed strength has since diminished to 5% ABV, and the beer has inevitably become virtually indistinguishable from its many mid-market rivals. San Miguel (Spanish for Saint Michael, so not to be confused as a Marks & Spencer own-brand) gets its proper name from the district in Manila where the original brewery was set-up over a century ago. The Spanish company we know today split from its Philippine owner in the 50s. Even after half a century the different beers they produce still share the same name and use a similar style typeface on their labels. The ship on the logo is a representation of the 1773 Spanish Navy 74-gun warship *San Miguel*. That ship was captured by the Brits and, just like the beer, the British embraced it as one of their own, re-naming it the *HMS San Miguel* in 1782. *GT*

SCRUMPY JACK
Scottish & Newcastle
UK, 6% ABV

Scrumpy Jack's origin lies in the obsolete dialect word 'scrimp', meaning a withered apple. 'Scrump' is the verb that was used to mean stealing somebody else's apples, but originally referring to the custom of collecting windfalls. A variety of locally-grown gems such as Brown Snout, Tom Putt, Foxwhelp and Chisel Jersey are used in the production of Scrumpy Jack; a proud and traditional drink, made in one of the oldest cider mills in the UK. A true amber cider, this is also one on the decline – courtesy of all the new trendier brands. Coming in at a fairly potent 6%, it isn't one of those flat warm real ale-types, but falls somewhere in between those and the sweet, fizzy stuff that you used to buy at the offie in your early teens. For me, it conjures up images of sitting lazily outside ye olde pub in the quaint village of Scrumpyshire on a summer's evening, a few locals and farming stereotypes scattered around, a friendly game of cricket on the village green... then a load of out-of-towners turn up in their X5s to do impressions of The Wurzels, and order bottles of fashion cider, pour it into iced pint glasses and discuss city living in their expensive education accents. There's always someone out to spoil the quintessential vision. Joe Strummer was from Somerset. I bet he never stood for such intrusions when he went back to his roots for a ploughman's and a pint of the good stuff. *SW*

SKOL

Carlsberg UK
Denmark, 3.2% ABV

Skol! Skol! Skol! Skol! In distant times known as the
1980s, when Skol pillaged the nation's pubs like so many
of its Viking forbearers, an animated Hagar the Horrible
invaded TV ad breaks with this catchy drinking song. In
the ads, a rabble of Vikings bang on tables and slop pints
of ale above their heads, chanting, *'Skol! Skol! Skol!
Skol!'* But Hagar's dim-witted pal Eddie doesn't join in.
'Why aren't you singing our drinking song?' asks Hagar.
Eddie pauses and replies, 'Erm, I've forgotten the words.'
Boom, and indeed, boom. But the ads were popular
staples of 80s TV, alongside those featuring the Smash
martians, the Hamlet cigar smoker, and of course good
old George the Hofmeister bear. Skol's tagline, 'Horribly
Good Lager,' is all too easy to make fun of, but the truth
is that Skol, like 80s rivals Carling Black Label, Harp
and Hofmeister, was horribly average. Fast forward to
the noughties, and the only interesting thing about Skol
is that it has survived. Since Allied-Lyons got out of the
beer business, Skol has been owned by Carlsberg, brewer
of, well, Carlsberg. So it is at least now owned by the UK
arm of a Danish company. However, unsurprisingly given
the huge promotional effort behind Carlsberg's titular
brand, or even that behind Tuborg, Skol has been
somewhat neglected in the marketing department and its
sales have subsequently slumped. Skol is a Scandanavian
word meaning a toast or salute. So here's to the UK's
second or third favourite Danish lager brand. *Skol! Skol!
Skol! Skol! PB*

SKOL SUPER
Carlsberg UK
Denmark, 9% ABV

I know of a man who complains that, 'Skol Super is just not the same as it used to be. They've ripped the heart and soul out it, basically, and totally watered it down.' Skol Super used to have an alcohol by volume percentage of 9.2%. It is now down to 9%. The man with the grievance is named Duggie, and he can usually be found sitting on a park bench in a bomber jacket shouting at clouds. Yep, Skol Super is not so called because of its super choice of barley, super blend of hops or for its super filtering methods. No; it enjoys the 'super' moniker because it is – along with the likes of Carlsberg Special Brew and Tennent's Super – one of the most potent super strength lagers around, with enough alcohol content to knock out a horse. Taste-wise? If I was being charitable I'd describe it as a robust or maybe full-bodied drink, with a slightly sweeter taste than you'd usually find in strong lagers, with a distinct fruity/floral character. If I was being accurate I'd nail it as the equivalent of drinking the contents of a flower vase that has been spiced up with some barley wine which has hitherto lain hidden at the back of someone's drinks cupboard for 20-odd years. In short: keep very much at arm's-length and once opened do not return to it. It may look harmless enough but it has the potential to take your face off. *TJ*

SOL

Coors
Mexico, ABV 4.5%

Like many others, I used to be a fan of Sol. A few years
back, Sol was the new kid on the block; the future of
bottled beer. It would be served in bars with a slice of
lime in the bottle neck and was a favourite among the
image-conscious who could afford to pose with it. They
would be gawped at and ridiculed by those drinking pints
of generic lager who'd pretend they didn't secretly crave a
bottle, all the while wishing they could cast away their
pretensions and go back to basics. Sol was first brewed in
Mexico by a German in 1899. No idea what he was doing
making beer there, but he called it 'El Sol', Spanish for
the sun. Since being the original poseur beer, it seems to
have been overshadowed in recent times by the likes of
Corona et al, mainly because they all taste nicer. Let's
face it, Sol is the kind of image drink where you get to the
bottom of the bottle and wonder what you were thinking.
No one was impressed and your palette lost all respect for
you. So to save face, you start telling those around you
that the idea behind the lime was to keep flies out back in
the old country. That's when one of your pint-quaffing
mates tells you the real story; it was to mask the smell
(and likely the taste). It isn't too offensive, but it's
certainly on the wrong side of pleasant. *SW*

STAROPRAMEN

InBev
Czech Republic, 5% ABV

The name of this Czech classic has been mispronounced by thirsty punters to bemused bar staff more times than I care to mention. Various attempts have been overheard, a favourite being 'Stop Amen'! The beer's tag line advertising itself as the Star of Prague is an easy way to remember pronunciation. (A direct translation of the name is in fact 'Old Spring'.) Most folks these days ask for it as 'Star' and they are served one of the greatest pilsner beers the celebrated brewers of Bohemia have ever created. They're not daft these Czechs; not only (in 1869) did they build the Staropramen Brewery slap bang in the middle of Prague's industrial quarter ensuring a proximity to beer drinkers, they also have a term, *riz*, which means 'just right' in the context of a thirst quenching finish to a beer. Using Saatzer hops gives Czech pilsner its distinctive taste and Staropramen pilsner especially that cutting, hoppy delicious finish. In the 1930s, the Staropramen brewery was the largest in Czechoslovakia, but after the Second World War all Czechoslovakian breweries were nationalised under Soviet rule. When independence returned in 1989, Staropramen became part of the Prague Breweries group (Prazské Pivovary). Although now a worldwide brand owned by InBev, weirdly, until the late 1990s one of the few places 'Star' was available in the UK on draught was in the Rovers Return at the end of the Coronation Street Granada Studio tour! Now say after me, '*Star-oh-Pramen* please, Betty!' *GT*

STELLA ARTOIS

InBev
Belgium, 5.2% ABV

The UK's favourite bottled beer is a contradictory tipple. On the one hand, it's 'reassuringly expensive' and promoted via arty European cinema-style adverts. On the other, it's widely and unpleasantly known as 'wifebeater' and associated with driving lily-livered drinkers to spousal abuse. Clearly overpaid marketing bods are desperately trying to rescue the brand's image by promoting it in exactly the opposite way than one might expect. After all, how many drunken wife abusers do you know who would appreciate a 30-second homage to *Jean De Florette*? The tactic seems to be working, as the beer gradually loses its (probably underserved) dodgy reputation. At 5.2%, Stella is stronger than some rival brands, but as rocket fuel goes it's not exactly Tennent's Super. It's strong enough to send an underpaid office drone stumbling into a gutter on a work night out, for sure, but probably not strong enough to drive any sane husband to domestic violence. Here's the history: First brewed in 1926, Stella was originally a Christmas drink named after the Latin for 'star'. The Artois comes from Belgian master brewer and Leuven brewery owner Sebastian Artois. The window design on the label is meant to reflect Flemish architecture, and the words 'Anno 1366' refer to the inception of the Leuven brewery. It's not unpleasant to taste – light but faintly hoppy – and it's easy to see why this is a no-brainer popular choice. But, really, there's nothing much 'premium' about this self-styled 'premium lager beer'. The adverts are good though. *PB*

STONES BITTER

Coors

UK, 3.7% ABV

Old warhorse Stones Bitter has been around since the
1940s when William Stones Ltd began to make the stuff
at the Cannon Brewery in Sheffield. Sean Bean worked
there – or at least his character did in the football
Britflick *When Saturday Comes*. The brewery was closed
in 1999, and Stones is now brewed by American conglomerate Coors in Burton-on-Trent. In its bright orange cans,
Stones is perhaps the EasyJet of beers. Pouring it into a
glass reveals a drink that almost exactly matches the
colour of the can. It looks fizzy, it looks weak, it looks like
Iron Brew. Stones was the first ever alcoholic drink I
tasted. I was seven and my granddad asked me if I could
pour him a can. I sneaked a little taste and promptly spat
the horrible poison back into his glass. Thankfully, he
didn't notice. But it got me thinking, what was the big
deal about drinking beer? It was horrible. Obviously,
since then, I have learnt the error of my ways and now
drink as frequently as possible. But I'm still no fan of
Stones. It used to be called Stones Best Bitter. Perhaps
the Office of Fair Trading had something to do with the
removal of the word 'best'. If I'm at a party and it's the
only drink there, I'll drink it. But I would then have to
ask myself, what kind of crappy parties am I going to
where people are bringing Stones Bitter? *JR*

STRONGBOW
Scottish & Newcastle
UK, 5.5% ABV

What is it with alcohol and advertising at the moment? Cider bestseller Strongbow has bucked the trend of using arty scenes of orchards and much-happier-than-me Irish folks enjoying a seasonal cider, and has instead gone down the leery-beery route favoured by Carling and WKD, with ads featuring gobby, matey oiks living life to full down the boozer. I want to drink Strongbow (made by HP Bulmer, as opposed to Bulmers Ireland, for S&N) as it retains an almost earthy, barely washed, gig-going coolness that, coupled with its cool, clean taste, makes it a very palatable drink, and a fantastic 50% ingredient of snakebite. But I do not want to drink it if – as the adverts suggests – I will become by association a great lumbering ox of a man, with more than a touch of the Munster in his gene pool, who cannot sup a pint of cider without a ridiculously drawn out 'look at me' sigh of refreshment. I mean, what was wrong with Strongbow's famous two arrows that twanged into the bar at the end of the old ads? And they were actually a historical reference. Hands up who knew the cider was named after Richard 'Strongbow' de Clare, the 2nd Earl of Pembroke? If you can ignore the new adverts, Strongbow is a reliable tipple. You will become far more blurry and fighty (it's 5.3% ABV), and tempered by recurrent and agonising bouts of acid reflux, but fear not, the advantages of Strongbow outweigh these piffling trifles. *Twang. Twang. SG*

STRONGBOW CIRRUS
Scottish & Newcastle
UK, 5% ABV

In the summer of 2006, something very strange happened: the sun came out for more than an hour and Britain melted. Hot and bothered drinkers turned to new and exciting beverage offerings – and millions of them bought pint glasses filled with Magners and enough ice to sink the Titanic. The ice age all came together perfectly in the balmy, sweaty heat of summer 2006, backed, it has to be said, by an aggressive marketing campaign. But one set of cider drinkers did not have their heads turned by that newfangled caper and they were the Strongbow drinkers – dedicated fans of an altogether earthier appley goodness. S&N have clearly spotted this, and introduced a kind of halfway house between Magners and Strongbow – a Frankenstein's monster called Strongbow Cirrus. The problem is that Cirrus is so watery, and so far removed from the original Strongbow brand that it actually tastes sweet. Sweet Strongbow, I ask you! Oh cruel, cruel fate, to be tempted by the green-eyed monster into making sub-par cider, which, in financial terms, may well unfortunately have some lasting effect on the original beautiful golden nectar. I mean, there's got to have been some extra money pumped into marketing the stuff, and where is that going to come from? God help them if they end up damaging the original Strongbow brand – I know some of those dedicated Strongbow drinkers, and there's no doubt they'll fight a good fight. *SG*

TENNENT'S

InBev
UK, 4.4% ABV

Reportedly Fred West's favourite tipple, Tennent's was the first lager to be brewed in Scotland, in 1885. The Wellpark Brewery was founded in Glasgow by Hugh and Robert Tennent in 1740. Originally called the Drygate Brewery (where it was based), it expanded some fifty years later when the family bought a nearby brewery and renamed the site. As Scotland's best-selling pale lager, Tennent's has enjoyed a number of 'first' accolades... the first draught lager in 1924, the first canned lager in 1935 and the first keg lager in 1963. And no doubt it is probably the first beer to touch the palette of drinkers in Scotland. And speaking of taste, I'll not bore you with 'true taste of Scotland' clichés or Irvine Welsh 'schemie' references; it's all standard in price, strength, taste and consistency. It is lager in colour and lager in taste and doesn't pretend to be anything else. A cool, quaffable tasty lager and at a medium strength, it will do the trick if you are out on an all-dayer. You can rely on the Big T; he's an old friend to reacquaint yourself with when you're in town. If you live in Scotland, it is generally as easy to lay your hands on as IrnBru or water. Or in the beer tent at T in the Park festival if they ever have a decent line-up and make it worth going to. Outside of Scotland, it's less in your face, but still available everywhere. *SW*

TENNENT'S SUPER

InBev
UK, 9% ABV

The mainstream beauty of Tennent's Super can be
conveyed by two numbers: 500 and 9. That's 500ml per
can and 9% ABV. Pretty good, but what does it taste like?
Once removed from the blue tube, Tennent's Super
becomes an all together different beast – a more docile
one, if you will. The consistency is as it should be; namely
the bubbles rise congruently and at an equidistant pace
for a good number of minutes. The colour is a rich amber
without the associated darkness of many other super
lagers. The first sense which is attacked upon raising the
glass to one's lips is the sense of smell. Traditionally the
sense of smell has been a poor second to the sense of taste
when used to make decisions upon various beers but, in
this case, the sense of smell is a valid weapon in the
super lager drinker's armoury. Once opened to the
outside air the smell of ham disappears completely
leaving just the pleasant floral aroma to ascend from the
glass. The lager fizzes kindly upon the tongue and then
the taste hits you. Hits you like a nuclear weapon. The
taste of Tennent's Super is unlike any other super
strength lager, let alone any other lager currently on the
market. Danger is what makes the world go round. If
man didn't take risks then man would still be living in
caves wondering why everything was so cold. Tennent's
Super is very much like that – it is a risk but one with a
big payoff. *TJ*

TETLEY'S ORIGINAL
Carlsberg UK
UK, 3.6% ABV

I've heard of people fantasising about being locked in a brewery but some people just have to go that little bit further. Harry Houdini was once submerged in a sealed metal cask filled with Tetley's Original, but for once, the task of freeing himself proved too great even for the famous escapologist and he had to be rescued from the barrel (moral: don't drink and dive). That was back in 1911, but Tetley's has been around for a lot longer than that having been brewed in Leeds since 1822. It likes to cultivate something of a down-to-earth Yorkshire air, and this is evinced by the numerous sponsorship deals which the brand is associated with, leaning heavily towards the sport of rugby; the implied message being: it's full-bodied, unpretentious and can hold its own against any namby-pamby soft southern drink. If it was a body part it would be a cauliflower ear. The bitter ale is still made using traditional brewing methods, such as dry-hopping of cask ales (adding the hops after the wort has cooled) and with Yorkshire Square fermenting vessels (producing a distinctively flavoured beer that is impossible to replicate with other factory methods), and the resultant hoppy flavour has a rather pleasant appeal. I've not yet worked out how many cans of Tetley's Original you would need to fill a metal cask a la Harry Houdini, but I'd strongly advise against trying to replicate his stunt. It would be a complete waste of ale. *RM*

TETLEY'S SMOOTHFLOW

Carlsberg UK
UK, 3.8% ABV

It's Tetley's, but it's smoother and creamier. That much is clear, as is the fact that UK drinkers buy more Smoothflow than Original. Smoothflow (like Creamflow or just plain Smooth) signifies that the beer is pressurised with nitrogen, either from a pressurised keg, or from a can or bottle with a widget. So let's nail this once and for all – what the hell is a widget? The word 'widget' itself means an unspecified or hypothetical good or product, often used in economics speak ('How many widgets would you need to sell to blah, blah, blah...'), and was first coined by George S Kaufman in his 1924 play *Beggar On Horseback*. Yes, I missed that one too. The widget found in a beer can was patented by Guinness brewers Tony Carey and Sammy Hildebrand in 1968. The first samples sent to Guinness in Dublin were labelled 'Project Dynamite', but brewery workers called them 'widgets', and the name stuck. The modern floating widget is essentially a small hollow plastic ball, about 30mm in diameter, with a hole in the top. As the can is sealed it is pressurised with liquid nitrogen, some of which is forced into the hollow widget. When the can is opened, the pressure quickly drops, and nitrogen and beer jets out from the hole in the widget, agitating the surrounding beer and creating a surge of tiny bubbles, which eventually settle to produce a smooth and creamy head. So Tetley's Smoothflow is part bitter pale ale and part scientific marvel. *PB*

THEAKSTON'S BEST BITTER

Theakston
UK, 3.8% ABV

The T&R Theakston Brewery is located in the town of Masham, North Yorkshire, which is handy for this reviewer as it's just around the corner from my house. There is something really special about a beer only travelling 500 yards before going into your glass – a fresh beer certainly makes a better beer in this case. T&R Theakston was founded in 1827 by Robert Theakston and John Wood at The Black Bull pub in Masham. The Theakston family owned the brewery until 1987, when it was acquired by Scottish & Newcastle. But, heroically, four Theakston brothers bought the brewery back in 2004, returning it to family ownership. Theakston's ales are widely available on draught in pubs in the north of England, and in bottles in supermarkets around the UK and in Germany and the USA. Best Bitter is the most readily-available of the five cask ales produced by Theakston, and is often described as a session beer, that is, several pints can be drunk over a 'session' of time without completely intoxicating the drinker. It's not too strong, yet a satisfying beer to drink. It does have a pleasant flavour – quite hoppy and distinctive, leaving an agreeable taste on the pallet. It is a dark gold colour, darker than most bitters, however, if you're a real bitter enthusiast, it will probably disappoint as it's only mildly bitter. Theakston also produces XB, Black Bull, Traditional Mild, and Old Peculier, but if you don't want a heavy night then Best Bitter is a safe and pleasant bet.
HC

THEAKSTON'S OLD PECULIER

Theakston
UK, 5.6% ABV

Old Peculier, or 'The Legend', is not for the faint hearted... This is a full-bodied, strong and very smooth beer – so smooth you can end up drinking more than you first intended. It's Theakston's most famous beer, and 'the beer that made Masham famous' – if you mention the town of Masham outside of Yorkshire, people will often say, 'That's where Old Peculier comes from,' – or at least that's what they often say to me. Why the odd spelling of peculier? There's actually nothing peculiar about it. A peculier is a parish outside the jurisdiction of a diocese, and the beer is simply named after the peculier of Masham. It's another beer brewed from the traditional fuggle hop by the family that has run the independent brewery for over five generations (excluding a short spell under S&N). The brewery has its own visitors centre, and the family's wealth of experience means they have more than a few interesting tales to tell. Old Peculier has a dense and smooth head which tops a dark body and is best viewed (and drunk) close to a log fire which shows off its amber highlights. It has a complex, quite malty taste, and although as a local I would say that it is best drunk within touching distance of the brewery, I can say with sincerity that it does travel well. But it is deceptively strong. So, wherever you choose to drink the stuff, it's best to make sure you're not in a hurry and have something soft nearby – to roll into. *HC*

TIGER BEER
Tiger Export
Asia, 5% ABV

This is a South East Asian premium lager beer from the home of the Singapore Sling, which, for the uninitiated, is a cocktail and not a weapon of mass destruction. Tiger Beer is well known to merchant seamen the world over and really should be mentioned alongside that other staple beer from that part of the world, Singha. Both are of a premium strength that creeps up on you before you can say 'knock' in a game of dominoes. Singha weighs in at a heavyweight strength of 6% ABV, while Tiger isn't far behind behind at 5%. Tiger's natural home in the UK is lurking in a Thai restaurant, as it is the perfect clean-tasting, complement to a green curry. Formerly only available in bottles, a draught variety arrived on these shores in 2008. Launched in 1932, Tiger is the flagship brand of the former Malayan Breweries Limited, now Asia Pacific Breweries. In the 50s, the Malay-based writer Anthony Burgess named his first novel *Time for a Tiger* after the beer's long-standing advertising slogan. The first edition of the book depicted a bottle of Tiger Beer on the cover. After publication, Burgess asked Malayan Breweries for a complimentary Tiger Beer clock, but was refused. However, in 1970, when Burgess had become famous, Malayan Breweries told him he could drink any of their beers on the house when in Singapore. 'But it was too late,' Burgess wrote in his autobiography, 'I had become wholly a gin man.' *MW*

TUBORG
Carlsberg UK
Denmark, 4.5%

Big news for UK drinkers: Tuborg is back, back, back!
And we hadn't even realised it had gone away! Yes,
Carlsberg UK, brewer of Carlsberg, a Danish medium
bitter pilsner, have relaunched Tuborg, another Danish
medium bitter pilsner. Carlsberg say they are both very
different, with the Carlsberg brand tasting of 'summer
apples and pine', and Tuborg tasting of 'flowers and
lemon'. I'm not so sure about that – to these cynical
tastebuds, they both taste like quite a lot like Skol,
another Danish lager from Carlsberg. Like Skol, Tuborg
was last seen as a 1980s no-frills watered-down version of
European lagers. The new version has a beefed-up 4.5%
ABV, but can it really be expected to compete in a
marketplace bossed largely by a very similar stable-mate?
Tuborg was first brewed in 1873, so it pre-dates Carlsberg, but is that enough to make UK drinkers clasp it to
their bosoms? What Carlsberg hope will differentiate the
Tuborg brand is the marketing angle. Carlsberg have
chosen to align the new Tuborg with live music, sponsoring a stack of UK festivals. Tuborg is already linked with
live music in Europe, having sponsored Denmark's
Roskilde Festival. And even in its previous life as a 1980s
'standard lager', Tuborg danced to a musical beat, with
TV ads including a particularly 80s big-haired spot
featuring Bruce Hornsby and the Range-style piano-
noodling, and a memorable *'Tu-Tu-Tu-Tuborg'* bargain
basement rip-off of Peter Gabriel's *Sledgehammer* video
(with voiceover from Chris *'Tiswas'* Tarrant). *PB*

TYSKIE
SABMiller
Poland, 5.6%

Regarded by many as the most – and some might say only – palatable Polish beer, Tyskie (that's *Tisk-yeh*) is closer to a Czech pilsner than any of its compatriot rivals, with a golden colour and a thick white head, and because of its infinitely smaller gut-rot potential, it's consequently its home country's best selling brand. Still brewed in the southern Polish town of Tychy – close to Katowice and birthplace of no less than Liverpool FC's clanger-prone former 'keeper Jerzy Dudek – this beer is part of a long and self-contained tradition dating back to 1629. Thanks to the influx of Polish nationals, however, it has quietly and subtly worked its multiple award-winning way into the pubs, hypermarkets and grotty corner stores of Britain. Strangely in a market usually hell-bent on world domination, Tyskie's overlords SABMiller seem perfectly happy to keep it as a parochial concern and currently offer very little in the way of English blurb to entice the casual internet browser or indeed make life simple for clever dick contributors to impertinent beer guides. Maybe they're trying to retain an air of mystery and east European otherness: who can tell? But by using a very helpful online Polish-to-English translator, it seems that the best way to appreciate Tyskie is as follows: *'Cover with beer hand – szklankę and aggressively zamieszaj. Discover next szklankę, but then, sweat it involve air fastly nose right now pestilence. Then, you will feel bouquet of fruit smell like bananowy, truskawkowy or jabłkowy.'* Couldn't have put it better myself. *MJ*

VICTORIA BITTER
Scottish & Newcastle
Australia, 4.8% ABV

The Aussies have got it all haven't they? Beautiful beaches, cities and girls. Fantastic wine, food and weather. But, just like the beer in question, I'm not bitter. No, seriously, Victoria Bitter is not bitter – it is in fact a lager. As the label depicts and Australian etiquette (sic) dictates, everything must be shortened to a colloquialism. A barbeque is a 'barbie', a kangaroo becomes a 'roo' and so Victoria Bitter is known as 'VB'. Many Aussies I know despise this beer as cheap, sugary, bulk-brewed blandness. Technically, they're not far off the mark, the Aussie conglomerate Carlton & United Beverages, who also make Foster's, haven't used fresh hops in the brewing process for many years, preferring to use hop extract because it's cheaper and quicker. No matter how it's made, VB remains an Aussie mass market favourite. Because of its fresh, not-too-gassy taste that is yeasty and slightly sweet, it goes exceptionally well with burnt meat. Aussies will buy their VB for the barbie by the case or 'slab', as they say. Sold mainly in chunky fat bottles known as 'stubbys', they can be drunk quickly therefore your beer stays colder, especially when your bottle is insulated in a neoprene stubby holder. In the UK you'll find VB stubbys being sold at pint prices in Aussie theme bars, but whether it's called bitter or lager just give thanks that they don't yet brew a Victoria Dark version or you could be heading to your mate's barbie with a case of VD. *GT*

WHITE LIGHTNING

Scottish & Newcastle
UK, 7.5% ABV

If you're a White Lightning drinker, the chances are that you are also eating from a bin and living in a hedgerow and probably wouldn't benefit from reading a review of it. Or you are too busy listening to Happy House music and smoking 'tac', and are incapable of reading anyway. However, I'll soldier on. It's made of fermented corn syrup. It's cheap. It's so sweet that your teeth are in danger of falling out after a mouthful. It's white cider. It's probably one of the worst drinks money can buy. I drank this once when I was absolutely brassic and needed to get skulled in an instant... and it was from Netto too (oh, the shame). There is no sophistication about this drink. You buy it in two litre bottles with one thing on your mind. There's no pleasure to it, no satisfying aftertaste and it shouldn't be served with dinner, or anything else for that matter, unless of course you are eating from said bin. When White Lightning was unleashed, it was originally only available in three litre bottles (for the price of two litres, kids!). In 2004, after turning the majority of the lower-classes into borderline alcoholics, Scottish Courage developed a conscience and stopped selling it in three litre bottles – meaning that fans of the drink had to fork out for two bottles at a time. And don't try pouring it into a pint glass with ice and pretend you have a job – you're not fooling anyone. *SW*

WOODPECKER
Scottish & Newcastle
UK, 3.5% ABV

Back in the 1950s, Woodpecker Cider was a pioneer of TV advertising, with ads featuring *Top of the Pops* faves the Beverley Sisters. In its 70s heyday it was *'Woodpecker Cider, Hereford Lighting, tastes so bright. Cool and crisp, sharp and light!'* The 80s and early 90s gave us hedgehogs squashing cars, ducks shooting hunters, and *'What a refreshing change'*. Fast forward to the noughties, and Woodpecker has disappeared from our screens and from public consciousness, with availability dwindling and sales plummeting. Everyone I know has a story about Woodpecker Cider playing a leading role in the events of their youth, whether it was the first pint they ever bought, or the reason they spent a house party puking down the porcelain pan. Brewed by HP Bulmer UK and now owned by S&N, Woodpecker has been around since 1894 but only came to the fore during the 1970s when it was first introduced on draught. The woodpecker on the logo is of the green variety, also known as a 'yaffle', like Professor Yaffle of *Bagpuss* fame. Times have moved on for cider drinkers: average strength has increased leaving Woodpecker's 3.5% ABV stuck in the past; fashionista clones now want their cider in bottles; the carbon offsetting mob want organic not mass manufactured; even the kids have turned to blue alcopops. I believe snakebite is the only thing keeping it alive which is perhaps a shame in this era of nostalgia. Go on, put on some flares and order a Woodpecker. *GT*

WORTHINGTON'S CREAMFLOW

Coors
UK, 3.6% ABV

William Worthington first brewed beer in 1744, building his own brewery in Burton-on-Trent. The town of Burton, blessed with plenty of 'good water', soon came to dominate the British brewing industry, with more than 30 brewers situated in the area. Rivalry was intense – none more so than that between William Worthington and William Bass. It was a battle of the Wills, if you will. Both became powerful peers, and it was claimed that their political funding led to the government offering favourable treatment to brewers. During one House of Commons debate, Lady Astor, the first female MP, commented, 'You might as well call it the beerage as the peerage.' William Worthington died in 1800, and was succeeded at the brewery by his son, also called William, and then by his grandson, another William. The rivalry ended in 1927, when the Worthington & Co brewery was bought out by Bass. Bass and Worthington are now owned by Coors, and the US company's UK head office stands on the site of William Worthington's original brewery – although Worthington's Creamflow is now brewed in Hampshire at the same Alton brewery as Carling and Grolsch. Creamflow, launched in 1995 using pump technology developed for Caffrey's, is smooth and cold, fruity and nutty, but bears little resemblance to William Worthington's brew. To get an idea of what that might have tasted like you'll need to try William Worthington's White Shield, a 5.6% bottle fermented IPA that's still brewed in Burton. *PB*

ŻYWIEC

Żywiec
Poland, 5.7% ABV

Do you keep giving this hugely popular Polish beer a wide berth because you don't know how to ask for it in the boozer? It's quite simple, using only two syllables. First, *Zhiv* as in *Dr Zhivago*. And then *yets* as in the involuntary throat spasms you make with your throbbing head down a Krakow hotel toilet and vague memories of being eight sheets to the wind the night before. *Zhiv-yets*. With its strength of 5.7% tasting more like nine or ten, Żywiec is triple-filtered to remove anything as namby-pamby as subtlety, leaving a golden brew that is slightly chemical on the nose, Happy Shopper loaf-like in the body, and with an aftertaste of freshly rusted nuts and bolts. Żywiec's gimmick is a heat-sensitive logo on the label that only appears if the beer is at the right temperature (+4°C), and disappears again when exposed to body heat. This is handy for checking that you're experiencing the optimum drinking pleasure, and also for proving to yourself that you're merely bored rigid in one of the dreary chain pubs that are its primary UK stockist, and not actually stone cold, toes-up dead. So, it's difficult to order, unpalatably bitter and worryingly addictive. Żywiec does, however, have one bonus feature that excuses it all: thanks to the exclusive use of the purest water from springs at the foot of the Skrzyczne Mountain (Pronunciation? You're on your own there, kidda.) it's reputed to be absolutely hangover-proof. I beg to differ. *MJ*

INDEX

ALSO FROM TONTO BOOKS:

THE BURGLAR'S DOG
ALTERNATIVE GUIDE TO DRINKING
IN NEWCASTLE UPON TYNE
Revised and Updated Edition
By Mark Jones
ISBN 9780955218392
Paperback, £9.99

A hilarious and irreverent pub crawl through Newcastle upon Tyne – STILL officially the eighth best party city in the world!

Meet the Burglar's Dog. He's angry and rude, he's got four legs and an abysmal hangover. His unique guide to drinking in Newcastle contains bleary-eyed reviews of more than 150 of the city's best and worst pubs, plus furry-tongued features on stag and hen weekends, pub DJs, toilet attendants, and other things that get up his snout.

An acerbic drinking companion, the Burglar's Dog cocks his leg at pub mediocrity. No target is too soft, no gripe too petty, no insult too cruel. Essential reading for anyone who has yet to find something even remotely 'to die for' behind the glittering façade of a luxury lounge bar.

Revised and updated to include new pubs and features!

AVAILABLE NOW FROM ALL GOOD BOOK SHOPS INCLUDING AMAZON.CO.UK AND TONTOBOOKS.COM.

SIN CITIES
ADVENTURES OF A SEX REPORTER
By Ashley Hames
ISBN 9780955632600
Paperback with colour photos, £7.99

With a weakness for women, good times and binge drinking, it seemed inevitable that television presenter Ashley Hames would turn cult hero with Bravo TV's highest-rating television show *Sin Cities*, blazing a toxic trail through a minefield of debauchery and fantasy across the globe.

His career began as the infamous L!VE TV News Bunny, before *Sin Cities* saw him hoisted up on meat hooks, tortured, clamped and generally trampled on in the name of entertainment.

In this book, Ashley investigates the sexual habits of some of the most extraordinary people on the planet – from the bizarre to the unimaginable – and somehow helps it all make perfect sense.

'Irresponsible, insane but inspired, the Queen should present Ashley Hames with a knighthood and a straight-jacket as this fine book amply illustrates that he is equally deserving of both.' - Piers Hernu

AVAILABLE NOW FROM ALL GOOD BOOK SHOPS INCLUDING AMAZON.CO.UK AND TONTOBOOKS.COM.

PARALYMPIAN
MY AUTOBIOGRAPHY
By Stephen Miller
Foreword by Kevin Keegan
ISBN 9780955632617
Paperback with colour photos, £9.99

Stephen Miller was born in 1980 with Cerebral Palsy, a brain condition that makes balance and co-ordination more difficult than usual.

One of Britain's most successful athletes, Stephen has won consecutive Paralympic gold medals at Atlanta, Sydney and Athens, plus dozens of other international accolades in the club and discus events. He has repeatedly broken both the Paralympic and World records in the club event – the Paralympic equivalent to the hammer.

A writer and poet, Stephen's inspirational autobiography tells of his struggles and triumphs, and is told with refreshing honesty and infectious humour. The book's foreword is written by Stephen's friend Kevin Keegan.

'I know how hard it is to compete at the highest level. It takes dedication, courage and self-belief, and Stephen has those qualities in abundance. His story is truly unique and inspiring.' - Kevin Keegan.